LIFE OUTSIDE THE GAME:
A Sex Trafficking Testimony

by

Tatiana Yoguez & Nicole McCall

with

Carla DuPont

Life Outside The Game: A Sex Trafficking Testimony

Copyright © 2021 by Tatiana Yoguez & Nicole McCall

978-0-578-93797-7

Cover Design: Richard Anthony Evans

Dedication

To Jessica S. Green, our beloved best friend and sister.

We'd like to thank God, our Savior, for His everlasting love and forgiveness.

I also dedicate this to my mother, Veronica. Thank you for being so hard on me even when it hurt because I don't think I would have made it this far without that motherly love and the seeds you sowed into me. I love you for being there no matter what!

Tatiana

Letter to our readers,

This true story contains strong emotional content with child sexual abuse and trauma that can be triggering for some who have similar experiences. We want you to be mindful of your surrounding energy while reading our story. Self-care after reading is encouraged, mentally and spiritually. If you have experienced being sexually exploited by family, a lover, a friend, or a stranger, and you would like guidance on how to navigate a plan to safely exit the life of sex trafficking, we are here to talk and show you a safe way to live outside the game.

xo,

Tatiana & Nicole

www.lifeoutsidethegame.com

LIFE OUTSIDE THE GAME:
A Sex Trafficking Testimony

Nicole lined her lips with a Beet lip pencil by MAC as she waited for the valet to skip around to the driver's side of her vehicle to open the door and hand her a valet ticket. She pressed her lips together, then smacked them to blend the color while looking in the mirror on the sun visor flap.

"How is your Sunday, ma'am?" the valet asked, smiling because he knew his tip depended on it.

"Well!"

"Great, here is your ticket. May I have your name and last initial," he asked ripping the ticket off a stack.

"Nicole M. Thank you," she took the ticket and

straightened out her skirt as she stood up out of her car. Just as she began walking toward the building, she heard a familiar voice.

"Nicole!" she spun around to see Tatiana, herfriend of almost 25 years.

"Tatiana!" she beamed and paused her trek inside.

Tatiana got out of her car, fingering her long, Dominican blowout in her reflection of the car's window. She was handed a valet ticket before quick stepping onto the sidewalk in front of the moderately nice event hall to meet her friend. They hugged and walked side-by-side.

"Once inside, they saw a step-and-repeat, a registration table, and a few ladies putting the finishing touches on the décor: vases of flowers on tall boys, signage, and balloons.

"Tatiana and Nicole!" they were greeted by a young lady. "Welcome! We are so happy to have you!"

"Thanks for the invite."

"We asked you to arrive a little early so we could let you get a feel of the place before the event. Let me show you to the main room where you'll be speaking.

Then, I'll take you to the sitting room."

They followed the young lady who walked like she was on a mission. She bee-lined into a room with several round tables, nicely decorated. At the front of the room was a long table on a riser with five chairs, two of which were certainly for Tatiana and Nicole.

"Here is the podium where you'll be speaking. If you want to walk around with wireless mics, we have those, too. We'll all leave the room for about 10 minutes so you can kinda talk into the mics and practice a little if you want." She smiled and walked out closing the door behind her.

Tatiana picked up one of the wireless mics to rehearse her intro into the empty tables and chairs that would soon be filled with teenage girls, their mothers and caretakers, along with advocates for sexual justice. "Human trafficking is a crime that forcefully exploits women, children, and believe it or not, even men. It is said human trafficking happens in every country around the world. Dosomething.org suggests there are between 20 and 40 million people lost in human trafficking today. That's a big number. But today, we aren't talking about the world; we are talking about our very own backyard."

She looked to Nicole, who nodded for her to continue, "The 2018 Federal Human Trafficking Report states that over half of the criminal human trafficking cases active in the U.S. that year were sex trafficking cases involving only children. Most of the children trafficked are between 12 and 14-years-old."

Again, she looked to Nicole, who had found another wireless mic to join in. "The two ladies you see before you...Tatiana and myself...we were among those children who were trafficked between 12 and 14-years-old. We were kidnapped, drugged, and sexually exploited for someone else's gain. To use a more common term, we were pimped out. Thankfully, we were in the .04% of survivors who are identified."

Tatiana put the mic to her mouth and made a loud "Raaaaaaaa!" sound to mimic a crowd's applause. They both laughed.

"Are you ready to tell them our story, sis?"

"I've been ready."

TATIANA

Jessica and I met in the sixth grade at school. After one class together, we just clicked. Perhaps the reason for our instant friendship came from our strikingly similar looks. We were both light skinned, had long curly hair, and similar builds. Kids at the school often confused us. It's not like we looked alike in the face, but they couldn't see past the complexion and hair, I guess.

"Oh...Jessica! There you go! What's up now?" I heard one of my peers sneering behind me while I stood at my locker. That tone of voice was all I needed to hear to know they were incensed. I rolled my eyes and exhaled deeply. *Here we go. Again,* I thought. Ready for a fight.

"I'm not Jessica, but I can be." I corrected, turning around so the girl could see I wasn't. I noticed a clearing in the hallway where instead of going to the next class, kids were forming a circle around me and the girl, who had a few other girls backing her up acting like they were really about to shake something. In middle school, there aren't that many shapes and sizes, but the girls were different heights. One looked like she ate greasy chicken wings for breakfast. I wasn't about to let them smell any fear.

A few kids cackled; boys put closed fists over their opened mouths to mask their excitement. Girl fights were always electrifying! When boys fought, it was about brute force. When girls fought, boys hoped a boob fell out or a skirt flew up. Instigating an already tense situation, I asked, "But what's up?"

That whole year was like the scene from *The Five Heartbeats*, "Every night I have to fight to prove my love!" Instead of the husband fighting other dudes off his wife, I was fighting classmates off my friend. She wasn't even there, but I was fighting for her honor, as well as mine.

Other girls were naturally envious of Jessica. She was opinionated and had no fear. Girl or boy, she didn't care who you were, Jessica had no problem speaking her mind. The boldness she portrayed, her pretty face, and young bangin' body is what caused many girls at the school not to like her. When Jessica walked in, people took notice. She'd walk into a room like, 'Yes, I'm here.' Her confidence is what made her stand out. You loved her or hated her; there was no in between.

Jessica's attitude and demeanor are what made her a target for pre-teen jealousy. That same jealousy is what I had to side with when defending us. Jessica, obviously wasn't in the hallway at the time; but I was also defending myself to show those little middle schoolers I wasn't no punk. This scene played out repeatedly through the school year. Especially as we became closer. We got to a point, like with most BFF friendships, if you saw one, you saw us both.

Our friendship poured outside school walls when, it seemed at a point it was me and Jessica against the world. Two cool girls hated for being attractive, something we could not control.

That's when I began venturing out of my neighborhood, traveling from the southside of Jacksonville to the northside to hang out with my twin. I was at the age where finding friends outside my immediate surroundings led to city and school bus excursions and having girly, pre-teen sleepovers. Up to that point, I was a normal kid with friends in the neighborhood from the local elementary school. Me and my little friends were adventurous, often using our vast imaginations to run the streets and play with each other until the streetlights came on.

There was a wooded area that encompassed my neighborhood, giving it more of a suburban feel. We'd teeter on the edge of the woods, using our vivid imaginations to make up worlds and games, then act it all out. One day while roaming, we found a house in the woods. Nervous to broach the house on our first adventure, we tip-toed around the house snickering and whispering, careful to shush whoever's voice was being too loud for fear we'd be discovered by the mean, old man who lived there. We conjured up a lumberjack-esque man, who would tower over us with a long, grey beard that hung over his flannel covered pot belly. We discussed him having a dungeon, a room where he tied up intruders after finding them stuck in the bear traps around his property. Never before did the crunch of dried leaves and fallen branches sound so loud under our well-worn play shoes.

Except, the day we ventured close enough to get a gander of the inside of the house, we discovered a family. A normal family. A husband and wife with a few kids. No mean ogre or a dungeon to be trapped in; no hunchbacks with missing teeth. A friendly family with more children to play with. Our adventurous pack's number grew and the fun multiplied. The mom fixed us snacks and welcomed our play in and around their house and through the woods.

As long as I made it back home before the streetlights came on, my mom was none the wiser. Nor did she care to ask where I'd had been or who I'd been with. As a single mother to me and my much younger brother, her energy was focused more on taking care of him and making sure the bills were paid. I mean not that I could blame her, my brother was so much younger that as a toddler, he needed more attention than I did. Still, as much as I understood why he got the lion's share of mom, I longed for some of her too.

When sixth grade approached, my mother enrolled me into a magnet school, Kirby-Smith Middle School of the Arts, which was on the eastside of town. Being so far away, meant the walks with neighborhood friends to school every day were exchanged for lengthy bus rides. I felt isolated on a bus going to a school full of 'big kids', none of whom I knew. Clutching my CD walkman, I enveloped myself in the sounds of my favorite groups Boyz II Men and Another Bad Creation CDs; crushing over ABC's heartthrob, Red.

Every day was more of the same, wake-up, be bused across town, zone out mentally playing out pre-teen fantasies, go to school, be bussed back home. I stared out of my bus window trying to put myself in a different headspace. I felt invisible, but I wasn't. Other kids would mess with me and girls would provoke me to rumble saying I thought I was "all that and a bag of chips" because I had pretty hair or asking where I came from as if I didn't belong on the bus the same as them. I didn't have to deal with this type of behavior in elementary school with the same friends and classmates I'd had since kindergarten. In this new atmosphere I wasn't invisible, I was a target.

When I looked at somebody, I saw them as a person. *You are you and I am me*, is what I thought. So those kids coming at me because of how light my skin was and the texture of my hair caught me off guard. Not only did I not know how to respond, I'd never dealt with that before. Instead of feeding into the negativity, I busied my mind counting clouds and finding cloud shapes to block out the energy of my environment. It's amazing how many shapes clouds can resemble.

During this time, I became a lonely child. After school, I'd go home and keep to myself in my room. My brother being seven years my junior made it hard for us to have a relationship beyond me being his big sister. I listened to the radio and CDs, instead of roaming free with the friends from elementary who went on to the neighborhood middle school.

Jessica coming into my life was a welcomed breath of fresh air. She was a friend at a time when I felt all alone. I rode home on the bus with Jessica from school or my mother would take me to her house. Being bused around town was no joke. I preferred my mom to do the driving; bus rides seemed to go on for hours and hours. Sometimes I'd fall asleep, wake-up, and still be bouncing along on the big, yellow cheese. Having my mom drive me around was more a privilege than a right.

Being that Jessica lived with her grandparents, they were not as strict on her as younger, watchful parents usually were. With the combination of natural coming-of-age enlightenment and Jessica's more lenient upbringing, I was coaxed out of my shell.

In the middle school environment, we start smelling ourselves, as the old people say. Having so many girls hating on us and all of a sudden getting so much attention from boys had us thinking maybe we were all that and a bag of chips. Maybe there was something to the light skin and long hair. Fueling each other's fire, we developed loose mouths that said just about any and every thing on our minds. We wandered through the school a lot, skipping classes and going to each other's lunch periods. That type of behavior landed us nearly permanent seats in ISS: In School Suspension. By the end of the school year, we were regulars in after school suspension as well.

We nicknamed ISS, ISSP which stood for In School State Prison because of the layout of the room. The room was setup like a voting poll station; big, oversized cubbies for one child to sit inside. Our views were blocked on three sides. The only thing we could do was write sentences, do homework, and look at the slabs of engineered wood where other schoolmates had drawn pictures and wrote taunting phrases in their own boredom. To us at 11 and 12-years-old, it felt like torture. Like a prison.

The principal had our number. Ms. Brown drove a pink Cadillac and proudly wore regalia of Alpha Kappa Alpha, Inc. She always signed us up for paddling. Jessica's grandparents were not having it though. They did not want their grandchild's butt to see the searing end of a paddle. Yeah, she needed a little attitude adjustment every now and then, just keeping it real. The grandparents refuted the paddling with proof of her intellect. Jessica was smart as a whip. All of her classes were gifted classes, but without one of her besties by her side, she felt incomplete. Jessica would dumb herself down, pretending not to know answers trying to get herself a ticket into my traditional classes so we could get into more mischief together.

Jessica and I knew we were often up to no good, but we still hated Ms. Brown for reprimanding us. We had a pact that we were going to egg and key her car when the school year was over for sticking us in ISS and paddling us, well me, so frequently. We didn't make good on our promise, though we were tickled as hell when we found out someone else actually had.

For seventh grade, we both left Kirby-Smith. Partly because Ms. Brown's angry antics barred us from returning. Jessica went to her neighborhood school, so did I. Instead of seeing each other in class every day and domineering our spot in the lunchroom, we tied up the phone lines at home for hours and hours each day on the phone.

NICOLE

Southside Middle is where I met Tatiana. We were sitting next to each other in the front office on September 10th, the eve of one of the single most tragic days in U.S. history.

"What did you do?" she asked making a little conversation. I'm sure she was halfway being nosey and halfway befriending a troublesome sista. Neither of us was happy to be there.

I looked down and waved my hands toward my body like I was presenting some sort of magic trick. I wasn't a tennis shoes and jeans type of girl. I preferred skirts and crop tops, anything girly. Undoubtedly, this was a distraction for other students, which got me unwanted attention from the teachers and administrators. Any trouble I got into was because I refused to follow the dress code. "You?"

"Arguing with a teacher," she answered. I smirked at my new friend. I knew she was a little on the wild side then.

We both probably thought we were going to get a slap on the wrist. Little did we know, we were about to be suspended from school when the school year wasn't even a good four weeks in yet. We chatted a little back and forth, trying not to let on that we were actually enjoying not being in class. We exchanged phone numbers while making small talk about getting in trouble, vowing to keep each other company while home over the next few days. Our other friends were going to be in school, so we needed something to pass the time away. We were too young to be running the streets; we could keep each other busy.

The next day was September 11th. We had plenty to discuss on the phone as the harrowing details of the tragic day's events unfolded. Airplanes flying around the northeast, causing havoc. We watched in disbelief as the second plane flew into the World Trade Center's South Tower, as well as its subsequent collapse. We were anxious and bewildered, knowing something really bad was happening before our eyes, not yet able to grasp just how monumental it was.

I was the middle child between brothers, all three of us had at least seven years between us. My parents divorced when I was only two, so for the most part, it was just me and my older brother in the house with our mom. We relocated from Oakland, California all the way cross-country to Jacksonville after the divorce.

By that time, my older brother was pretty much an adult, being in his late teens. He didn't really want to be bothered with his almost teenage sister. I suffered the loneliness of also having a mother who was rarely home. My mother's energy was put into having a revolving door of male companions. She didn't make time for us, nor did she pay attention to me as her single daughter in the home. My mother worked and had an active dating life which meant her attention was not on raising her kids or being supportive of our interests and education. That forced me to grow up quickly to manage my young life on my own. I had to keep myself on track because my mother was distracted with her steady rotation of different boyfriends.

When my mother was home, she wasn't attentive, and having a brother who was so much older left me with a lot of time to do whatever I wanted. Whatever leash I had was the one I put on myself. Like my new friend, Tatiana, I involved myself in imaginative play. I imagined a full family with parents who were together instead of facing the ugly truths that my father promised to visit and spend time with me, then reneged on his word. He promised to pick me up, then left me sitting on the steps of the porch like the cliché scene in movies. I'd also pretend I was playing with a host of siblings so I wouldn't be lonely or bored.

For a period of time, it seemed the only people who really showed me attention were my grandparents. As a youngster, they often took me on trips with them to almost every single state in the country. They introduced me to their friends and other family members, giving me a much different landscape than being home alone. My grandfather built a treehouse in the backyard for me, so I spent a great deal of time there. I enjoyed camping and wandering around my backyard.

Tatiana gave me much needed social interaction. We really bonded during our suspension, as well as having a mutual friend in common. Now, she had somebody to relate to, a kindred soul to mesh with. We had similar problems at school and were happy to have someone we each could share that with.

At some point, Tatiana blasted in her usual upbeat tone, "Oh my gosh! You would love my friend, Jessica!" Back in those days, there was no such thing as social media. The coolest technology we had were cordless phones with caller ID and three-way features. Tatiana hooked it up, introducing us over three-way. When she did, I was surprised that just like she said, Jessica and I got along like homegirls who'd known each other since forever. The clique was instant between the three of us.

Every single day, we raced home from our bus stops with one goal in mind...hop on the phone to dish about the latest gossip going on in our seventh grade lives. We'd close ourselves up in our rooms with Jacksonville's latest hip hop radio station playing in the background to drown out what we were saying, as if we were spilling some serious tea. It's not like anybody in any of our houses was paying us attention anyway.

Outside of the phone, we hadn't had the chance to hang out in person. I saw Tatiana in the hallways and when one of us skipped class to chat it up in the lunchroom for the other's lunch period. Jessica, being all the way across town meant we didn't get to see her at all. Our only connection to her was on the house phones getting to know each other.

That didn't stop us from constantly planning to get together. At times it seemed like an obsession. We'd have our daydreams about what it would be like when we finally saw each other. We made grandiose plans to go places and do things. We even picked our matching outfits. I don't know whose money we planned to use to go any of the places or do any of the things we planned. Or maybe that wasn't exactly a part of the plan. But as pre-teens with little to no means of steady transportation and even less means to money, we just had to wait to get together in person. Time flew by, with our birthdays all in a row. Even with staggered month birthdays in September, October, and November, we still had not managed a meet-up. I guess turning 12 and 13 didn't really call for a celebration, huh? A balmy, Floridian Christmas came and went.

Finally, on New Years' Eve, our trio hooked up. It seemed like a lifetime in teen years! It was the first time we'd all been together. I invited the girls to my spot, where my brother had also invited some friends over to kick it in his makeshift studio. We all took advantage of the holiday since our parents and grandparents were also celebrating the incoming year. I don't remember where my mother was, but we were home alone.

"Oooh! That's my jam!" one of us would squeal every time a new video came on. We spent the day watching BET's Notarized Top 100 Countdown of music videos of chart toppers during the course of 2001. Tatiana grabbed a hair brush off the dresser and belted out tone deaf melodies like she was trying out for her 15 seconds of fame. Me and Jessica fake boo'd or applauded based on just how intentionally bad she was. Jessica snatched a jacket and a hat from my closet for her performances, trying to fully embody her inner celebrity. I was the dance queen, booty shaking and p-poppin'. On the songs we all loved, we fell over each other like in the game Twister, trying to out dance each other or dance the routines on the videos that we knew so well from watching them over and over at least a hundred times.

We spent a little time outside in the cool, crisp, Florida air as the countdown into the New Year led to a barrage of fireworks. Beautiful streams of red, white, and blue exploded in the sky. Yellows, greens, pinks, and purples, too. Even at that age, where we thought we were too old to be fascinated by fireworks, we were still mesmerized by the bursts. Caught up in the festive atmosphere, we hugged each other, happy to finally be together. We lit sparklers, laughing and joking as we wrote the names of the boys we had crushes on in the air. As the clock struck midnight, gun shots rang out observing the holiday. The New Year celebration was a magical time, one of the only times the world seemed to stand still. I was happy to have found a pair of girls who, already at such a young age, seemed more like sisters than friends.

I had no idea how a chance meeting with Tatiana

in the front office would lead me down a course that would forever change my life, as well as theirs. When I think back on that whole day, our laughing and joking is like a slowed down celebration scene in a movie. The kind where everything is happy and seems perfect; everyone is getting along and life couldn't get any better. The very definition of calm before the storm.

TATIANA

Those same lil' boys whose names were written in the air with sparklers were the same lil' boys who had their minds blown. Puberty had already began making changes in our little bodies, especially our minds. I would be a lie if I said we weren't all a little boy crazy. Nicole and I saw each other's crushes in school every day, but Jessica had to describe hers to us. We got more than our fair share of attention from boys at the school. It seemed like the more the boys called out to us in the hallways, the more the other girls hated. Or vice versa.

Neither of us had any boyfriends yet, we weren't quite to that level of dealing with the opposite sex, but we were ready to take it there. The year before, I'd been on the city bus and school bus riding across the city, so I felt big and bad enough to use that as a mode of transportation. I was tired of being stuck at home while my whole teenage life passed me by during Christmas break.

"Hey girl, what's up?" I called Nicole first. Being that we went to school together, she was more easily accessible than Jessica.

"Chillin', girl. What's up with you?"

"Nothin'. Man, I'm tired of being in this house!"

"Me too! I'm sooooo bored. I never thought I'd say I miss school but..."

"Whoa! Whoa! Whoa!" I interrupted her laughing. "I wouldn't say all that. Girl, chill. We just need to find something to do."

"If school was back in session, we would have something to do."

"Ugh! The only thing I miss about school is seeing Beard's cute face," I swooned. Just saying his name sounded like magic to me. I loved the way 'Beard' rolled off my tongue. Beard was in my math class. It's like he cast a spell on me whenever I saw him. I could barely hold it together when seeing him sent butterflies fluttering in my belly.

"Don't nobody want Beard but you!"

"That's a lie and you know it!" we both laughed. "I wanna go to the mall." *Beep.*

"Me too." *Beep.*

"Jessica is calling now. Let me tell her we're gonna call her on three-way."

I answered the call, then told her I was going to call her right back so we could take part in our new, favorite pastime.

"Hola chicas!" Jessica yelled into the phone.

"Look, girl, we're trying to go to the mall. You down?" Nicole got straight to the point.

"Let's do it. I just got my hair done, too? Oooh, you know I'm 'bout to be killin' it! They ain't ready to see Ms. Jessica!" We all laughed at her wild shenanigans. It was just Jessica being Jessica. We agreed to meet at the mall. "I've been so bored, too. This is perfect. What time are we going?"

"It'll take a little while to get ready," Nicole started. "Then we have to find a way to get there."

"We can take the bus if we have to. I don't mind the ride," I said.

"Oh, now you don't mind?" Nicole teased.

"Not when it's getting me out of this house!"

We made our plans to meet up at the mall. We weren't the only people who had the idea to go to the mall. There were a good number of teens there, probably spending the little money they got for Christmas or just itching to have somewhere to go like us. As we wandered around, we ran into some boys we went to school with. It was a relief to see familiar faces. I was hoping to see Beard, but I didn't.

We sat in the food court for a time, people watching and jonesin' as others walked by us. There were five or six of us, so safety in numbers made us bold enough to crack jokes and not feel threatened. We were less concerned with starting trouble and more focused on just having a good time.

We took turns talking about our exciting or bland holiday experiences, what we got, what we didn't get, and what we wanted. We chatted about the teachers we loved and those we wished wouldn't return when school started back the following week. We window shopped, even tried on clothes that we knew we had no intention on buying in the spirit of having a good time.

In a fake English accent, Jessica said, "Hello angels. You sure look beautiful today." We tried on sunglasses and posed in front of the floor length mirror like we were on the film poster for Charlie's Angels. I wrapped a fluffy, yellow boa around my neck, and Nicole put a wacky teal, leopard print hat on her head. Clearly things we would never be caught dead in in real life.

"No! That's not what he says!" I retorted, then started in my own phony accent, "Hello angels. You beauties are going to have the eyes of all the boys in school."

"*Annnnnt!*" Nicole sounded a buzzer, "Wrong! Mirror, mirror, on the wall..." we all burst out laughing.

"Wrong story!" I shouted. We took off the unpaid-for merch and ran out of the store.

After we separated from the boys who went to our school, we saw another group of boys. One of them had the hots for Nicole. At first, she didn't notice him; I did, though.

"Nicole," I tried to get her attention under my breath. She looked at me in response. She was more quiet than I was. "That boy behind us in the Starter jacket is staring at you."

"No, he's not," she turned around immediately to see. He was. "He is!" she giggled.

"I told you!" I proclaimed and burst into a fit of laughter.

"What do you think he wants?" she turned around and he was still following and still staring.

"What does any other boy want?"

"Girl," Jessica started. "Fling your hair, then smile a little bit. Give him something to look at." Jessica had all the confidence in the world. It was so infectious.

Nicole started to fool around with her hair. She took a deep breath but filled with young, teenage jitters, she started laughing instead. "Oh my gosh!" she laughed letting out the deep breath she'd just inhaled.

"He already likes you, you're halfway there," Jessica encouraged.

"I don't know what to say."

"You don't have to say anything," Jessica coached. "Let him do the talking."

The boy quickened his pace and tapped Nicole on the shoulder. She tried to hold it together, yet couldn't help but laugh. Me and Jessica stood there with our backs to her like we were looking in the store nearest to us so she wouldn't look in our faces and laugh even harder. It didn't matter. Between her being shy and having the laughing bug, Nicole ran the boy off.

We'd been in the mall for hours. I was ready to leave the mall; yet, not ready to go home. We bundled up in our jackets and walked into the outside world.

NICOLE

After me and my girls left the mall, we ended up at another friend's house. We hung out there for a while then decided to walk back to my house. By this time, it was dusk, we were back on the sidewalk headed home.

Jessica and Tatiana were both more outgoing than I was. I had my moments of being 'out there', but I mostly laughed at the two of them. They were two peas in a pod. It was so funny watching them interact. In a way, it's like we were all only children seeking the attention we found with each other. I was just more reserved than they were. They skipped and danced their way down the streets and sidewalks. I was a step or two behind, laughing my butt off.

Then they imitated me in the mall. A boy approached me trying to talk to me. They replayed that scene with bravado!

"Hey gul!" Tatiana started with a fake, deep man's voice.

"His voice wasn't even that deep!" I yelled to them ahead of me.

"Hey gul!" she did it again with a slightly higher voice. "I'm tryna get yo digits, gul!"

"Oh no!" Jessica mimicked. She brought her shoulders tight into her body and put both hands over her face, beating her eyes rapidly. "I can't! I just can't! AHHHHH!" then she took off running, flailing her arms in the air.

We all doubled in laughter. I knew they were picking on me. Coming from my friends, my new sisters, I didn't mind. They had every right because I couldn't get it together in front of him.

A car approached coming up the street towards us. It slowed as it got closer to us. "Hey, y'all looking cute. What y'all getting into tonight?" the driver asked leaning over. He looked to be a little older than us. Well, a lot older. He was already driving.

We looked at each other, then back at him. He wasn't imposing, nothing about him stood out until he asked the next question.

"Y'all going somewhere. Where you goin'?" That's when I saw the flash.

"Home," I answered. He was looking directly at me.

"Ok, ok. I see that, ya know," he sucked his teeth them broke out into a wide smile. He had a mouth full of gold teeth that flashed against his dark skin. So, he really was older.

At 13, some of my classmates bragged about having older 'men'. Especially, in the locker room when we were changing for gym. It seemed to be the main topic of conversation. Who was dating who. The girls who were claiming they had boyfriends in high school seemed to get more respect from the rest of us. Those high school boys were much more developed than the awkward, pimple faced boys we saw everyday. Later on, I'd find out they were just as awkward in high school because puberty hits everybody at a different time. From my vantage point, I saw more handsome faces, chiseled jaw lines, swag when they walked, and bigger, stronger bodies.

The driver started chatting me up and Jessica had a conversation with the guy in the passenger seat. Tatiana kinda stood there trying to see what we were going to do. This was my chance to redeem myself. Not only was he coming on to me, but he was older too. This was going to get the girls off my back about the young boy from the mall. Although, I wasn't sure if I'd ever live that down. I needed to tap into my confidence to give attention to people who gave attention to me. Attention was something I was desperate for and didn't even know it. Jessica had given me pointers on what to do once I had their attention. So, fling my hair and smile a little bit I did.

He seemed nice and we weren't ready to go home yet. Jessica seemed to have a good rapport with the other guy, so we looked at each other and shrugged. For a few minutes, it was all giggles and talking slowly. Nothing about this situation stood out to us as being the wrong thing to do. It wasn't like a man luring children into his van with promises of candy and stuffed animals. They weren't wearing shades, hats, and trench coats. They looked like regular, everyday dudes. I was 13, I knew what a kidnapper looked like. These guys were not kidnappers.

"It's kinda cold out there. Why don't y'all hop in with us?" he smiled.

I can't speak for the girls, but my mind was blank. It was getting colder, especially with the sun setting. Floridians don't do cold very well. What we consider cold, those up north wouldn't even flinch at. Floridians don't like wearing jackets. Jacksonville in January required at least a windbreaker.

I didn't think 'yes'; I didn't think 'no' either. Tatiana nor Jessica objected. Still, I'm sure he knew we were too young for him to be asking us to get in the car with him. That didn't matter to me at the time. I was flattered to be getting attention from a 'man'. They didn't ask again. Assuming our silence meant consent, the passenger reached into the back to open the door from the inside and we piled in.

Just like someone switched on a light, the atmosphere changed. They locked the doors. Not that we could get out of the car if we wanted to. At first, I thought he was being a safe driver. I guess that was wishful thinking. Being grown, we just hoped in the car not really thinking about the dangers that could potentially lie ahead of us being in a car with guys we didn't know.

"You girls are coming with us. We ain't lettin' you out," the driver said. His voice was no longer the sweet sounding voice he had when he initially called us to the car. I didn't know what to say, nor did I know how to take what he'd said. I'd heard older boys were more forceful or serious. As long as me, Tatiana, and Jessica were together, I knew we'd be ok.

TATIANA

What? Did this fool just say he wasn't letting us out? I wasn't ready to go home, but I didn't want to be kidnapped either. Dang! Kidnapped is a strong word. I don't think that's what this is. Maybe not kidnapped, but what the hell is going on here? This is crazy, my thoughts were running wild. *Calm down, Tatiana! Calm down! Whew, nothing is going to happen. Wait...did the doors just lock? Oh...my...gosh! Oh my gosh! As soon as we get to homeboy's house, I'm out. I'm taking off. If I start running, the girls will run with me. I can't tell if he's playing or being serious. Maybe I'm trippin'. We could have some fun together. Naw, I better get my ass outta here! Run to the first person I see and call my mom.*

The whole vibe shifted. The driver seemed to be coming on to Nicole so hard, then the energy changed as soon as we got into the car. Looking back, I recognize it's because their intentions were never good. Once we were in the car, they knew it was going to be hard for us to break away. They became cold. The conversation stopped. So much for being chatty, getting to know us better.

The driver putting the car in park halted my thoughts. I felt like I hadn't had a breath since he said he wasn't letting us out. I didn't know what that meant. Snapping back into consciousness, I looked out of the window to see a rundown hotel. Motel was more like it. *What is this place?* There were only two types of people who booked rooms like those: truckers, who longed for a few hours of sleep more comfortable than inside the sleeper of their semis, and people hooking up for quick sex.

There was no way this was going to be the fun time we wanted. I mean, I wasn't ready to go back home yet, but this? I would have taken almost anything but this. This was not going to be my idea of a good time. Whatever was waiting for us on the other side of those rickety looking doors was something I wanted no parts of.

"Let's go. And don't try nothin' stupid. Just walk," he said in a very direct tone. The swoony voice he'd given before when suggesting we got into the car with him was completely gone. We followed him to the room; he already had a key. That stood out to me. He led us into the room and his friend followed us in. We were sandwiched between them.

Just as horribly cheap as the rooms looked on the outside, they were equally as shabby on the inside. There were two beds and the floors were hard. I remember the floor being so hard it felt like the thin, decades old carpet was sitting directly on top of the concrete slab foundation underneath. The paint was a drab, vomit yellow and the bedspreads looked like something that was probably on my grandmother's bed 20 years before. The window treatment was a thick flannel, holding in the stench of sins committed in that room over the years.

Jessica went to sit down to chill, still unaware of the seriousness of what was about to go down. The bass in his voice jolted her back up as soon as her butt hit the mattress. "These are the rules. Don't try to leave this room. Don't try to look out the window. Don't scream or make any noises."

"Please let us go," I begged.

"Let you go?" he asked in a high-pitched voice laughing. "Now why would I do a thing like that?"

"I am 12!"

"Don't you raise your voice at me girl!" he boomed.

"I am 12," I corrected, trying not to sound as desperate as I felt.

"Ok and..."

"We're underage, not even teenagers."

"You wasn't too underage to get ya fast asses in my car. You knew what this was."

"We didn't. We thought we were just coming to hang out with y'all. Please just let us go and we won't say anything to anyone. I promise we won't try to get y'all in trouble."

"My grandparents are going to be looking for

me...for us," Jessica added. "I'm only 11. I gotta get home soon."

"Eleven?!" me and Nicole yelled.

"Ain't nobody goin' nowhere! Y'all my girls now. Eleven...12...however old y'all is."

Our eyes glazed over as we looked at him. We had no idea what was happening. We just stood there, almost at attention for what seemed like several minutes but was probably only a few seconds. He wasn't the type of dude to mince words, it seemed.

"C'mon Squeaky, we gotta hit it," his passenger said. *Squeaky...so this fool has a name. Squeaky? What the hell kind of name was that? And where did he even get a name like that? What grown ass man answers to Squeaky?*

"Aye cuz. Calm down wit' all dat," Squeaky responded with a hand motion for his passenger to chill. He didn't seem too upset that we had his name. Alias. Street name. Whatever.

Squeaky peered out of the drapes, moving them slightly. "Take ya clothes off." None of us moved. We were still frozen in place trying to figure out how we ended up in this predicament. Too scared to move. Too scared to make a peep. Damn near too scared to breathe. "I said, take your fuckin' clothes off!" he shouted. Instantly, we started moving. So fast that his passenger snickered, covering his mouth with his hand to stifle the sound.

We peeled our clothes off and let them *thud* on the floor. We were standing close enough to feel each other's body heat. Our closeness wasn't needed to keep us warm. Even as the chill in the air hit my body, I felt the heat of fear wash over me. I noticed Jessica was trembling next to me. I grabbed her hand and held it. I'd never been naked in front of anybody before. Nobody but my mom and my doctor. Had never even considered being naked in front of anybody. For what?

"Bras...panties...everything. Take it all off," Squeaky demanded. Hurriedly, we slipped off our undies.

"Oh yeah," his passenger said eyeing us, rubbing his hands together. I didn't understand what he was doing. I think that meant he liked what he saw. He circled us like a shark in bloody water, looking us up and down. Inspecting the freshest catch.

"Nice, right? Look at these puffy nipples. We got

'em just in time." *Just in time for what? What did that mean? What was wrong with my nipples?*

I looked down at my chest in a way that I'd never looked at it before. I was being sexualized. It's one thing to be sexualized by teenage boys who look and run, or make awkward comments I had to think twice about what they meant before they took off into a sea of other preteens. Or even be grazed 'on accident' walking through the hallway. The rudest, "Damn girl, your titties look good today!" didn't make me feel as dirty as I felt when hearing I had puffy nipples from this deviant.

I looked at my nipples and wondered what the puffiness meant. I had no idea. Nor had I ever noticed them before in that way. I was just happy to be able to fill in a bra that was bigger than an A cup. That was an accomplishment at 11. I wanted to cover up so bad. I wondered if that was the insatiable urge to cover herself Eve had after biting into the forbidden fruit.

Squeaky went back to the drapes. He looked to the left and looked to the right. Then he nodded at something or somebody outside. "I got people out there watching you." He turned around to us. "Don't try to leave. Don't try to call for help," he walked over to phone and yanked it out of the wall. "We'll be back."

When they left, they took every ounce of pride, confidence, and self-esteem we had in us. Opening the door caused a cold rush of North Florida's wintery night air to envelope us whole. The same way the streets were about to.

The feeling they left us with was utter fear. There is no other way to describe it. In our youthful ignorance there was no way for us to know that more than likely he was pulling our legs. We believed what he said. We believed there were people watching the room to see if we pulled back the curtains. We trusted that if we tried to leave the room, someone would see us and bum rush us to keep us there. He was not omnipresent, we knew that. It didn't resonate that he really could not be in all places at all times.

The feeling of fear totally consumed us.

NICOLE

Squeaky closed the door when he and his passenger left. I don't know if he closed it or slammed it, but it seemed to shake the windows. The sound reverberated through our naked, prepubescent bodies. We stood there for a minute or two or three. Tatiana and Jessica were still holding hands. We didn't know what to do. With that quick interaction, he'd instilled complete fear in us. How could it be possible for someone to make you fear them within the span of 30 minutes? How could they make you feel so insignificant? So miniscule? He had shaken all of us in less time than it takes to watch an episode of The Cosby Show.

I heard her breathe. Jessica. She took in a deep inhale, the sharpness of it filled the room. It was the only sound to be heard. Then she began breathing quickly. Her breaths got shallow and irregular as they quickened in pace. Maybe we all had been holding our breath. She started shaking like a dried-up leaf on a dying tree being blown in the wind. I pulled her into my embrace. We were all nude, but that didn't matter. I don't think any of us noticed, really. It wasn't anything sexual, I needed her to know I was there with her and that she wasn't alone.

Tatiana hugged her from the other side and she broke down. Her whole body shook as she had an emotional release of the weight that the three of us felt. "I'm only 11."

"You were serious?" I asked.

She nodded her head vigorously. I guess since I met her through Tatiana, I assumed she was my age or 12 at least. We were only two years apart, but at that age, two years is huge in terms of maturity and puberty.

That's when I realized I was the oldest of the bunch. As we stood there clutching each other, fearing for our lives, our safety, and the unknown, I felt a greater sense of responsibility. *How was I the oldest and the most shy? Had this been my fault? Was I supposed to protect them, us, from getting into mess like this?*

"We have to get out of here," I whispered. It seemed like an oxymoron that I was daring enough to want to hatch an escape plan, yet still whispering in case they could hear me.

"How?" Tatiana questioned.

"I don't know. We gotta put our heads together."

"He said people are watching the door...and the window."

"And he broke the phone," Jessica pointed to the wall where the defunct phone had been ripped away. She wiped her eyes and turned to face us. We stood in a triangle or sorts, clothes in piles around our ankles on the floor. Not once did either of us contemplate putting a single item of clothing on. Call it fear or determination, our minds were not on our nudeness.

"Do you really believe he has people watching us?" Jessica asked us.

"He said he did," Tatiana added.

"What if he's lying?" I asked. Up to that point, we had not questioned or challenged anything he'd said or done. Squeaky appeared to have his passenger marching in line to his orders, too.

"What if he's not," Tatiana challenged. "I don't know that we can test that right now."

"What will happen if we don't? We don't know what's waiting for us when he comes back. We have to try. I'm not trying to find out what's gonna to happen to us if we stick around here. It won't be good. I promise."

"All we wanted to do was hang out," Tatiana murmured out loud to herself. She wasn't blaming anyone, but I still felt that this was somehow my fault. Why didn't I stop us all from getting into the car? What was I thinking getting into a car with strangers. It's not like that was normal behavior for me. I hadn't done anything like that in my life. I didn't think it was normal behavior for them either.

"So, this is what the hair fling gets me, huh?" I tried to make a funny. All we each could muster was a *hmph*. "I'm willing to step over to the window to see."

"No!" Jessica said urgently. "We gotta stick

together. If one moves, we all move."

"C'mon!" I insisted.

"I don't want to move over there," Jessica said.

"Tatiana. What you trying to do? You wanna just sit here and wait to see if somebody is really out there?" Tatiana's eyes got big and she looked down. She didn't like the idea of being a tie breaker. She was the youngest among us. Perhaps that played into how she felt. She was also the only one of us who'd cried. I didn't think that disqualified her to make the decision. As far as I was concerned, all of our lives were hanging in the balance. I was ready to die trying to escape. "Forget this," I said and started easing toward the window.

I took one step, then another, then another. I took a deep breath and closed my eyes to calm myself. I took another step.

"Don't do it, Nicole," Tatiana whispered.

"I'm just going to pull it back a little teensy weensy bit." I was a pro at it. My mother and brother left me home alone so much that I'd perfected the art of looking out of a window without being seen. I'd stand right next to the window and barely move the drapes so I could see who was banging at the door when I was home alone. It was usually the mailman or my brother's friends. Either way, I didn't want anybody to know I was home alone.

I took one more step toward the window, toward our great escape. Then, I heard feet shuffling outside. Lazy walkers who didn't lift their feet when they walked. I leapt back to where the girls were and tried to breathe like normal. I realized we'd been standing in the exact place Squeaky left us. That's how scared we were. I heard talking and walking, the sound of plastic.

"Please, please, please, don't let it be them," I begged. I wanted my opportunity to peek out the window to see if our fear was unfounded or legitimate. I couldn't bear the thought of taking whatever kind of treatment they were going to dish out without us even trying to free ourselves. In their absence, I had grown bolder.

The sound of a key being pushed into the door had never prompted such a reaction out of me before in life. It felt like my heart seized in my chest. It was them. They were back. That was so fast, I didn't think they'd gone anywhere at all. They probably just went to sit in the car to see what, if anything, we would try to do. I was grateful, then, that I hadn't carelessly opened the door or been rash enough to yank the drapes back.

"Ohhh lookey what we got here!" Squeaky broadcasted to the dudes who followed him into the hotel room. This time, there were two new faces. It didn't take a genius to figure out what was happening. "My girls are still standing at attention!" he laughed; so did they.

He motioned for us to sit down, which we did all together. We huddled on the edge of one of the beds. All three of us looking at something different. Our eyes were darting all around the room. We didn't want to get any surprises. We could tell what was going to happen, but I didn't want to get smacked around or knocked upside the head for them to get what they wanted.

"I got something for you ladies," Squeaky said getting comfortable. He took his jacket off and tossed it on the back of one of the raggedy, wooden chairs next to the equally tattered wooden table. He sat down and opened the bag. There was a bottle of Hennessy inside, with some red cups. He used his finger to count the number of people in the room, then unstacked that many cups. He poured a swig in each cup and passed them around the room.

While he was doing that, one of the other guys turned the TV on to break up the silence in the room. The guys began making small talk around us, then tried to engage us a little. I wanted to scream. How could they want to talk when we were sitting there completely naked? We were crouched together, the three of us. Didn't they care that we were being held against our wills? Didn't that count for something? Anything? No? They wanted to coax us into feeling like being held against our wills was an ok feeling to have? They didn't want us to beg for our virginity, a gift almost as precious as life itself. They didn't want us to beg for our freedom. They wanted us to talk to them so they felt better about stripping us of something whose value we didn't fully grasp yet. They did. They knew how precious the gift was that they were about to snatch from us. No, there was nothing to talk about.

"Drink up, girls." By then, Squeaky had handed the three of us our drinks last. He pushed the bottom of the cup to make us drink faster for good measure.

Brown liquor. Talk about burn. Well, I can't say it was the brown that did it. Any liquor would have had the same effect on me at 13. Liquor had never crossed my lips. This was all so foreign to me. It burned my throat and everything else all the way down. Jessica started coughing a little bit; the guys laughed. I didn't find anything funny. I wondered how many other girls they'd done this to. They probably didn't even know. They seemed to be so comfortable sitting around us like that in that environment. Their small talk and drinks didn't help to loosen us up any.

Next, Squeaky pulled out a little baggy with white pills. "Here's one for you," he said taking one pill out and holding it over my lap. When I didn't move, he nudged me and exhaled his frustration encouraging me to stretch out my hand. "One for you and one...for... you..." he said doing the same thing with the other girls. Jessica was the last to get a pill as she was on the edge of the bed. We still had Tatiana sandwiched between us. They didn't wait for him to nudge them. They extended their hands when he approached them. "Pop 'em girls."

"Pop 'em girls," one of the guys mimicked Squeaky. He spoke like he was treating us to a shopping spree at the mall where we could pick out whatever we wanted.

"What is this?" I asked. It certainly didn't look like any of the meds I'd seen my grandparents take. Other than being frightened, I felt fine. Why did I need to take any pills?

"Candy," he responded and they all laughed. "Wash it down with the brown."

That's what he told me to do, so that's what I did. We were outnumbered and out muscled. There was no way out. I figured if I played nice, and the girls did too, we would be released and sent on our way. I'd much rather deal with being put on punishment, if that was going to happen, than be subjected to this madness. At that point, we just had to do what was necessary to get out of that room.

One of the guys sat next to me. He started rubbing my arm and, using a little force, pushed me to the top of the bed away from the girls. He sat down beside me and began kissing me. Not on the lips, but on the face and neck before making his way down to my chest. It was a weird sensation. Under different circumstances, I probably would've been open to it. Even through the nervousness of being with a boy for the first time, it would have felt good. Not this one. It felt like his mouth was made of sandpaper.

He tried to kiss me on the lips. I didn't kiss him back, but I didn't push him away or turn away either. He laid me back on the bed and motioned for me to get under the covers while he took off his jacket and got comfortable. My mind went blank the moment I saw him smile. He was about to enjoy something that would begin the process of killing me inside.

He slid between the sheets with me and maneuvered his way between my legs. All of a sudden, I felt something hot. I must have jolted because he asked if it was my first time. I nodded yes and he smiled wider. "Relax," he said breathing hot breath on my neck. He smelled like his day had been a long one. "You'll like it." Then I felt a searing pain. I jolted again, my eyes wide open from the pain. I slowly turned my head toward the headboard. He was going to like it, but I certainly was not. Wasn't even going to fake it. He grunted and moaned, not caring that his boys were right there acting like they were trying not to watch us. That was impossible.

I felt weight shifting around on the bed near my head. The sound of Jessica's sniffling increased. They'd chosen her next. I prayed that this would be over soon and he would get off of me.

TATIANA

Just go along with it, Tatiana. Just go along with it. Nicole was lying in the bed facing the table near the window. When the guy rolled off of her, she turned over, rolled into the fetal position, and hadn't moved since. Jessica was still under the covers going through her turn.

Her whimpering turned to crying turned to pleading. "Please no, please…please don't do this."

"Shut the fuck up and quit crying like a damn baby," the guy slapped her. He stunned her silent. I saw it all through my periphery. I was stuck on the edge of the bed where Jessica and Nicole had been taken away from me.

I was praying for a miracle. I needed something to happen. Maybe someone had heard Jessica begging and the police were about to charge through the door. They were staging a rescue on the other side of that door. I just knew it!

I wanted the cops to bust down the door and shoot every last one of them point blank range in the middle of the forehead. I knew the chances of that were about the same as seeing a pig fly. A girl could be hopeful, right? I needed an act of God to come and perhaps burn the building down. Yes, a fire. I needed the building to catch on fire and the fire alarm to sound so they would have no choice but to give us our clothes and vacate the room. Then me and the girls could run away into the night. Or into the arms of police and firefighters.

I wonder what'll happen if I tried to make a run for it. He didn't put the chain on the door. I can bolt towards the door, unlock it real fast, then make a run for it yelling and screaming. They'd be so scared, they'd run

out of the room and leave the girls in here alone, afraid
someone was going to come to see what's going on.

"Y'all wanna have some fun?" he asked. None of
us responded. We exchanged looks between him and
ourselves. He looked like a kid in a candy store. He
jumped on the bed and began singing, "London Bridge is
falling down, falling down, falling down. London Bridge
is falling down, my fair lady." *BOOM!* He plopped in the
bed laughing.

He sang the song again and jumped into the bed
with me. He went back and forth singing the nursery
rhyme, each time it ended falling in one of the beds. He
was so tickled, he kept laughing like a crazy person. We
weren't laughing at all. We were watching him, afraid. It
seemed like at any moment, he was going to stop and do
something to hurt us. It was that feeling where
something happens and you're waiting on the other
shoe to drop.

There was nothing fun or calming about him
singing his nursery rhyme to three naked girls being
held captive in a hotel room. It gave me the chills. The
sound of his laughter began to give me chills. There was
something so unsettling about Squeaky, even beyond

his taking and holding us. It's as if he honestly believed we were going to be ok joining in this display of debauchery with him. Eventually, realizing he was singing and 'playing' by himself, he grew weary of us being a non-participating audience.

I felt a hand on my shoulder. My time had come. Why me? Why us? I smelled something weird in the air. Between them drinking, smoking, and pill popping, I didn't know what it was, but it smelled familiar. Blood. The smell was blood. Like cows to slaughter. I could smell the blood in the air. I knew I would be sacrificed next.

Just go along with it, Tatiana. Just go along with it.

"Don't you make a fuss like your friend. Just lay here and go along with it. The girls go crazy over my shit," Squeaky bragged.

"Damn right, cuz!" one his boys agreed. *Then you go to them*. It was only a thought. I couldn't dare be brave enough to say that out loud.

This was not what making love for the first time was supposed to be like. In a room surrounded by strangers, and my friends even. Feeling tipsy and high from drugs I was forced to take. That's the difference between rape and lovemaking. There was no love here. In truth, I didn't know anything about sex or lovemaking. I only knew what I saw on TV and in movies. It never looked like this. I never saw a movie where girls were held and given liquor and drugs, outnumbered by double, then forced to have sex all together. I didn't know what this was or why it was happening to us.

He rubbed his dry, crusty hand down the front of my body. When he moaned, I winced. "*Mmm hmm*," he said licking his lips. I turned my head so he wouldn't kiss me. The thought of him feeling good with what he was doing to me, made me nauseous. My stomach shook as waves of nausea threatened to come up. I had to put myself in a different headspace and quickly before he did something to me.

Clouds. I took myself to the long bus rides across town to go to school. I was alone there and I felt alone here. I closed my eyes and imagined I was on the bus. Even being in such a torturous environment as being on the bus getting picked on and singled out was more welcoming than where I presently was. I tried to imagine a beautiful, blue sky illuminated by the sun's light filled with fluffy, white clouds. The clouds moved by to make way for other shapes. It was amazing how something as simple as an imaginary cloud in the shape of a tree calmed me. I saw shapes and animals, even one that looked like Beard. *Ahhh,* Beard. Then my thoughts shifted to envision his handsome face sitting in math class. And walking down the hallways. And at lunch. Any thought of Beard was a good one.

I felt a shudder. Squeaky started shaking. I thought something was wrong with him. I pushed him up while leaning back, forcing myself deeper into the cheap, uncomfortable mattress trying to put some space between us. My arms weren't strong enough for the weight I felt when he seemingly collapsed on top of me.

"Damn boy!" one of the boys said loudly, startling me as he slapped Squeaky's back. He slapped Squeaky so hard, we both shook on the bed. "She a good one, huh?"

"Yes indeed," he answered still leaving all his weight pressing down on me. After a few minutes, he collected himself enough to get off of me. The waves of nausea continued. I jumped up and scurried into the bathroom and threw up in the toilet. Hearing the sound,

Jessica and Nicole came rushing to my aid. It was next to impossible for us all to fit into that bathroom, but we did. One of them closed the door.

"Are you ok?" Jessica asked rubbing my back as I still leaned forward unconvinced I didn't have another upchuck inside me.

"I guess."

"It's over now," Nicole encouraged. "We're done." There was a faint sense of relief that we had all done some sort of sick, twisted duty. Performed an act we had given little thought to committing in our normal lives, if ever. Our sacrifice would go unnoticed and probably forgotten by those who demanded it.

"You think so?" Jessica asked.

"I hope so. They got what they wanted. I hope they just leave now."

"Tatiana, you're bleeding!" Jessica whispered in an urgent tone. We all looked down and there was blood at my feet. Then Nicole and I looked down at our own feet, then again at each other's. We all had blood somewhere. On our legs, thighs, or feet. We grabbed washcloths and used the sink to run warm water so we could wash off. The feeling of the warm washcloth soothed the pain I felt down there. It hurt so bad. I couldn't wait for them to leave so we could go home.

NICOLE

I was so sore down there. I had never felt anything like it. I felt throbbing. I tried to wipe myself gently as to not further irritate the area. The other girls were sore, too. I heard them wince in pain when they touched themselves with the washcloth. I wanted the blood off me as quickly as possible, but without making the throbbing worse.

I rinsed my washcloth. I watched the blood run down my hands and into the sink. The pink water gathered in the basin of the sink because the drain must have been somewhat clogged from decades of usage. I wiped and rinsed again. More blood, more pink water.

I was hurt and confused. I didn't understand why out of all the girls in Jacksonville this had happened to us. Well, why it had to happen at all. Weren't there girls who wanted to have sex? The guy on Tatiana said the girls loved him. Why didn't he go find one of them?

We walked out of the bathroom, all of us having washed up. Still naked, we all hunched over hugging our bodies with our hands. Of course, they didn't cover us. We needed to feel like we were preserving a little dignity. One arm stretching across the top and the hand opened flat to cover the bottom. We bee lined for our clothes which had been moved to the dresser next to the old TV. I grabbed our clothes and Squeaky stopped me.

"Naw," was all he said. I froze. Instead of turning around to look at him, I lifted my head slightly to see his reflection in the mirror. He looked at me with a straight face. Testing the waters again, I moved bringing my hand and the clothes toward my body. "I said, naw. Leave that shit right there."

"We can't put on our clothes?" I asked standing

erect having turned my head towards him. I was really confused. They'd gotten what they wanted, still, they wouldn't let us get dressed.

He walked over to me pulling up his pants which had slid to below his butt and yanked the clothes out of my hand. "No clothes."

"You're gonna make us walk out naked?"

"Who said anything about you leaving?"

"Huh?" I asked more as a reflex. I wasn't really asking, I was processing what he'd just said.

"Who said anything about y'all leaving? You my girls now. Yeen goin' nowhere."

My eyes slammed shut. I felt my whole body droop. This could not be happening.

"What do you mean *your* girls?"

"Mines!" he yelled. I still didn't get it, but I wasn't about to ask again. "Now move! Ya daddies ain't glass makers," he referenced us standing in front of the TV. They couldn't see through us.

"If you'd let us go, you wouldn't have to worry about us." It seemed like a simple solution to a simple problem to me. They got what they wanted, stole the most valuable thing we had to offer. *WHACK!* Squeaky slapped me so hard, I thought for sure I'd see half of my face on the ground. Jessica grabbed my arm and pulled me back to the bed where she and Tatiana were.

Squeaky made it clear to me that he did not like his authority challenged and he did not have a problem hitting females. In my mind, I saw myself hauling off and charging toward him at full speed screaming to knock him and the chair he was sitting in over to the ground. My own mother didn't put her hands on me. What made him think he could? And did? I wanted to hurt him. Feelings of confusion and hurt were replaced with seething anger.

"You can chill all that out. Ya ass ain't going nowhere and ya ain't doin' nothin' 'bout it! So just sit ya ass down!" he said responding to my chest heaving up and down rapidly. My frustration mounted as I tried to keep my mouth and my hands under control. I was definitely not a fighter; that was Tatiana and Jessica. This was just too much for me.

His boys didn't stand up to him to protect us or look out for us. They were pussies. Squeaky was smaller than all of them and he was running them. Three girls in the room had just been raped of their virginity and not one of the dudes would even try to stand up to him for us so we could get out clothes back. They'd just gotten their rocks off. They should've been feeling good enough to try to get him to treat us better. What did he want to keep us naked for?

We were outnumbered, so there was no point in us trying to rush him. I was going to have to keep my eyes peeled for an opportunity to get us out of there.

"Give 'em a little something to sip on!" He barked, "It'll take the edge off!" One of his do boys jumped to grab cups and poured a swig of Hennessy in each, then handed the cups to us. Squeaky stared at us, leaning forward until we drank it. There was something so dark and sinister about his stare. It was all dark, there was nothing else there. No life. No happiness. Even when he smiled, his eyes just looked dead inside. Beady, shifty little pinpoints in his head.

The other guys left the hotel leaving me, Jessica, and Tatiana in the room alone with Squeaky. As they left, they gave him dap and told him variations of they'd see or talk to him later. He didn't seem to mind being left behind. In fact, it seemed like he preferred it. Now, he was outnumbered. We could have easily taken him. I couldn't risk jumping on him without having the girls' support. Without us being able to talk about it, I didn't know if they would jump on him with me if I took the initiative or be frozen in fear that something would happen to us. They believed he had people watching us. Maybe the watchers were in the next room or just outside, close enough to hear him yell for help. I couldn't risk it.

"Me and my girls," he said smiling wide. His gold teeth shining in his mouth. "You and you," he pointed to me and Jessica, "get in that bed. You, over here with me. Nighty night time, girls." Tatiana looked at us like she wanted cry, but she didn't. Reluctantly, she got off the bed where we were and walked towards him. Equally as grudgingly, me and Jessica got into the bed where we were.

As I pulled the covers back, I saw blood stains on the sheets. Seeing them sent waves of pain reverberating through my body thinking about how just an hour ago, it felt like knives poking me in my vagina. My gaze met Jessica's as she saw the same stains. We both frowned up our faces, knowing we didn't have a choice in the matter. We positioned ourselves tightly against each other and pulled the covers over us.

I was determined to stay up longer than Squeaky to get out of there. Even if the other girls were asleep, I could run to get help and bring the cops back. There was no way the police wouldn't believe my story with me running the streets butt naked. I had to outlast him. I was the oldest. Not only could I not let him win, I had to protect my girls. We all had to get out of there. I was sure I could creep over the carpet and open the door without him waking up. He was laying on the side of the bed closest to the door.

I felt myself fading. I was so tired, we'd had an adventurous day. Some good, some horrible. Like a baby fighting sleep, I was trying to think of something to keep myself awake. It must have been the liquor and the pills. Still, I fought to keep my eyes open in the dark. Well, it wasn't completely dark; the TV was still on. That was going to be even better for my escape attempts. The sound of the TV would drown out my footsteps on the cold, hard floor. I could tip toe, really...I could... I could tip...I...

TATIANA

I woke up the next morning and at first was confused about where I was. I saw Jessica and Nicole, then realized we had been left alone. I sat up in the bed quickly and went to pull the cover back when I heard his voice.

"Morning beautiful," he said. I looked at him and the burst of hope I had popped like a helium balloon. Still trapped. I'd gone to sleep in hell and woke up there as well. I allowed my body to plummet to the bed. That was a mistake. It was nowhere near as soft as my own bed. There was no bounce. Instead of a few mini bounces, my body fell flat.

"Girls! Get up!" he said rousing Jessica and Nicole. They moved slowly, I guess we all woke up with the same sentiment. "Breakfast is on its way! But first, let's have some of this."

That statement meant we were not leaving. We were his prisoners another day. Squeaky held out a handful of pills. There were enough for us each to have two. He offered his hands to me first. I took one pill and a line of cocaine; he motioned for me to take another. I exhaled deeply, then grabbed my second helping. The girls followed suit. We downed the pills with Hennessy, then sat back on the bed.

His do boys brought us breakfast sandwiches from a fast-food joint and stayed a while. I vaguely remember them taking turns with us again. I guess that was their payment for being gracious enough to bring us breakfast. They came and went, so did Squeaky. We were never left alone though.

Nicole didn't even try to have a hushed conversation about breaking free again. There was always somebody right there and they'd scared the daylights out of us. Their presence just felt so ominous and overwhelming.

"Put ya clothes on," he ordered. I tried to stifle my excitement. We were finally going home. By that point, we'd been missing for a full 24 hours. The sun had set again, so I figured he thought it was safe enough to drop us off somewhere without being seen. We eagerly picked-up our clothes. They were wrinkled from being balled up and stacked on top of each other near the TV. I didn't care how unkept and unloved we looked; I'm sure my girls didn't either. We were just happy to be fully covered again. Any other time I would have turned my nose up at day old, wrinkled clothes. That day was altogether different.

As we got dressed, I kept my head toward the ground. I didn't want him to see me smiling and take it personally that I was eager to leave. I didn't want him to make us drink more liquor or take the clothes back off and take another round. Or calls his do boys to have their ways with us.

"Don't try nothin' stupid," he ordered as we exited the hotel. We followed him to his car and all piled in. "You, get in the front," he said to me. I don't know why he singled me out but that was the third time. I was the one he deflowered, I was the one he slept in the bed with, now I was the one in sitting in the front seat with him.

My family is from New York. When my mom moved to Jacksonville, we stayed in one area. It wasn't until my 6th grade school commute and meeting Jessica that I ventured outside of our small area. Riding around with Squeaky in the car was like me getting a tour of the city. All I knew were my immediate surroundings, so the tour he took us on, for me, was like being out of town.

At one of the stop lights, he tapped some white powder onto a closed fist, "Sniff this."

"I don't want to." I was green, but I wasn't dumb. I paid attention during all of the 'Say No To Drug' campaigns and the commercial with the fried egg that claimed, "This is your brain on drugs." I was already feeling impaired from whatever the pills were that he'd given us and the swigs of brown he routinely poured in our cups. I didn't want anything else to further diminish the way I felt.

"Bitch! I said sniff this shit! Now!" I knew better than to challenge him. I knew he wasn't above smacking us and, on top of that, he was driving. I didn't want to make him more upset being behind the wheel. I sniffed it.

We pulled up to a huge building that looked like a warehouse. With the snap of a finger, as soon as he put the car in park, men surrounded the car. It's like they magically appeared. The front. The back. The sides. They instantly began talking amongst themselves, "Oh, I want her."

"She look good."

"Naw fam, I want that one."

"That one is mine."

They were picking us. Scared. Confused. Worried. Even more than the night before, I was scared for our lives. I had never seen or been a part of anything like that before. There were so many guys and they all wanted their piece of us. I shook my head trying to remove the haze of pills, liquor, and cocaine from my mind so I could see more clearly. I was becoming more dazed. I could see and hear, but I could not react and what I would remember going forward started to fade.

He got out of the car, closed then locked the door behind him. "He better not leave us out here with all these guys," I whispered turning my head slightly towards the back seat.

"He won't," Nicole said. "It's too many of them."

He leaned against the car and talked to the guys for a minute, then got back in. I wanted to ask what that was all about. I couldn't. By that time, it took all I had to keep my eyes open and hold myself up. He left the parking lot of the building and turned the corner. We drove for what felt like the blink of an eye and we were in a neighborhood.

He pulled up to a house and parked. *What now? Why didn't he take us home? Or drop us off so we could find a way back home? Who lives here? Who's house is this?* He turned the car off and proceeded to get out.

Apparently, we were moving a little too slow for him. "Get the fuck out! What y'all waitin' on?" The question was rhetorical. All I saw were the golds in his mouth flashing as he spoke.

We walked in and there were guys already inside. I didn't recall seeing many more cars when we pulled up, but I wasn't exactly paying attention either. More guys came in after us. The house was long, not wide, kind of like a trailer. So, to the right was a long hallway with rooms. It seemed to go on for a hundred feet. That must have been the haze settling in.

Squeaky grabbed my hand and walked to the left to get out of the doorway. One guy grabbed Nicole's hand and took her down the hallway. Another guy grabbed Jessica's hand to lead her down the hallway.

She instantly reached out for me with her other hand and hurriedly whispered to me, "Tati, if I don't come out in five minutes, come get me." Then the guy snatched her away.

"Ok," I said squeezing her hand to let her know I heard her.

Squeaky sat me on a couch, that had seen better days, where I had a clear view of the door Jessica went in. With so many guys in the house, I knew it was only a matter of time before I was chosen, although it seemed like Squeaky reserved me for himself. My attention was drawn over to the TV. There was a huge, floor model TV that took up almost the whole wall it sat in front of. People were having sex on the TV.

Never before had I seen people having sex. I had not been introduced to porn. It seemed so taboo for me. I was partly intrigued and partly disgusted. Being in a house surrounded by men having my friends being forced to have sex against their will turned my disgust up a notch. There was no way I could watch people willingly having sex and enjoying it, while being held against my own will.

I looked around the room. I was scared. I didn't want to make eye contact with anyone, but I did want to see them. I felt if I made eye contact with them, they would think I was interested and would grab me by the hand. I just sat on the old, tattered couch with my arms crossed counting the shoes that lined the room. I kept loosing count, so I'd start over with my count.

The effects of the cocaine were hitting me hard. My thoughts didn't consist of much. I just remember being really high. My mind was in another place. I don't know how long I was sitting there, but it was much longer than five minutes. All of a sudden, Jessica came to my mind. I jumped up with a sense of urgency and ran to the room where she'd been taken. He didn't have enough time to grab me.

I found Jessica balled up on the bed crying. The only light in the room was the light from the hallway that slightly illuminated the space.

"You forgot about me!" she yelled.

"I'm sorry! I'm sorry!" I said rushing over to her. She wanted me to hold her and wanted to push me away at the same time. She cried harder. She was inconsolable. "We're leaving! We're leaving now!" I walked into the hallway, "We don't want to be here! We are ready to go!" I tried to demand.

Nicole came out of the room she was in and Jessica started to get herself together. She was still crying, but she'd put on some of her clothes. The three of us shuffled toward the door and stood in front of it. The guys around the room starting looking shook. They acted like they didn't know we were forced and drugged to be there.

How did they think this was something we wanted? We weren't smiling and laughing and flirting. We weren't cute, dressed like we were going on dates or trying to pick up guys. What part of our appearance and attitudes gave them the impression that we wanted to be there?

"Naw man, I'm out." One guy said. He walked up to Squeaky with his hand out.

"C'mon nah!" Squeaky said trying to convince

him not to leave. The guy looked at us, then back at Squeaky with a look that said he was not playing. He extended his hand out further and Squeaky gave him some money. Then Squeaky had an attitude.

That's when we realized we were being sold. Pimped. Prostituted. Suddenly, it all made sense what was happening. That's what he meant by saying we were his girls.

I was older when I put two and two together that he took us out of the hotel room because we were costing him money instead of making him money. I don't know whose house it was, but it was bigger and the rooms provided privacy. It was also harder for us to do anything to get attention inside of the house. In the hotel, we could yell and scream and made it be known that we were in there. In the house, there was a lot less likely chance we'd be heard. Apparently, having us in the house was more cost effective for him.

NICOLE

Squeaky told Tatiana to get in the front seat with him. I don't know what that was about. We wanted her in the back with us, but I think it was a control thing. If we were all in the back, we could bolt from the car at a light or if he slowed down. With her in the front, even if me and Jessica got out of the car, he could hold on to Tatiana physically restraining her. I mean, we rode with the doors locked, but kicking out a window wasn't far from my mind. He knew we wouldn't leave her. We were all or nothing.

We rode around for a while. It was like he was showing us around the city. Seeing the sights around Jacksonville was not what I wanted to be doing. I wanted him to slam on breaks and dump us on a corner. Any corner. And let us run for our lives.

I stared at his reflection in the rearview mirror. Man, the thoughts running through my head were crazy. I just wanted us to go home. I wanted to be free. None of this made any sense to me. We were just walking home from a friend's house, then we were being raped in a seedy hotel room. He made no announcements about where he was taking us, but it wasn't anywhere that would lead us back home.

He gave Tatiana a bump of something. She resisted; she didn't want to take it. He made her. The fire in his eyes when she pushed back scared me. I thought a meaner, more monstrous version of him was going to emerge. I think that was the first time he called one of us out of our names. He was making it very clear that he was in control at all times. What we ate, or didn't. When we took drugs. How much. When we had to drink. When we had to give up our bodies. What we put on, if anything at all. It was all in his hands. He treated us like he was our father. Except, aren't fathers supposed to teach their children things? Take care of them? Protect them? Keep them away from harm instead of introducing them to it?

As the streetlights moved in and out of the car, we were getting further and further away from home. He whipped us around in the car like he didn't care about his life or ours. Well, we already knew he didn't care about ours.

He pulled into a strip club parking lot. Of course, I'd never been to one; but, I knew what it was and what went on there. A queasiness overtook my belly. I could not fathom taking my clothes off in front of a room, no, a building full of strangers. That was going to be beyond humiliating. How in the world did he expect us to get on the stage and strip? And then he would take all of the cash? Was everybody in Jacksonville in on this kind of stuff or had we ventured into some underground layer?

The stuff I heard girls talk about at school was regular teenage stuff. Liking boys, first kisses, touching, occasionally a few fast girls were having sex. We spent more time fawning over famous boys and young men in groups whose songs we replayed over and over after we recorded them from the radio than we did talking to the boys in our faces everyday. We cared about our hair, our clothes, and which lip gloss was the shiniest. I never heard locker room talk about stripping for money. I never heard whispers of girls being kidnapped and held against their will. I didn't eavesdrop on conversations about being forced to take drugs. What level of the game was this? A strip club?

I was determined to make the best of this situation. If this fool was going to take us to a strip club, I was going to let it be known that he was holding us hostage. I had talked myself into doing a PSA from the stage or running up to a bouncer asking him to call 9-1-1 or even telling a guy I gave a lap dance to. Somebody was going to know I was not ok with this and I had not been home in over 24 hours. I needed this nightmare to end.

As we rolled to a stop, we were surrounded by guys. There were so many, I didn't know how we'd be able to make it inside the building without being overcome. Squeaky wasn't big enough to control all of those men. It was just him and us. He may have had a reputation that garnered him respect. That was evident by the way his do boys jumped at his every bark. I doubted that respect was enough to keep over 20 men from jumping him and taking us.

They started pointing inside the car. They were snickering and staring at us hard. I looked at them all. My gaze went around the car and around to each of them. Some of them licked their lips at us. One blew a kiss at me when we made eye contact. He wanted me to pick him. Instead of being like the others saying which one he wanted, he wanted one of us to choose him. That was a smart tactic. Some were raunchy, grabbing onto their crotches. As it was urban culture not to wear fitted clothes, sagging was really in during the early 2000s. It was not a stretch to say if a few of them pulled down their pants one more inch, everything they had to hang in their boxers would spill over their pants.

I felt Jessica shudder. We were disgusted. Me and Jessica were looking all around us, Tatiana was just there. She wasn't really moving; she was out of it. I couldn't tell if her eyes were open or closed. All I knew was, if she was out of it and Squeaky was pre-occupied with trying to help her walk arm-in-arm, he wouldn't be as aware of what was happening around him where me and Jessica were concerned. We'd have to fend for ourselves.

Squeaky got out and stood beside the car for a bit. He was talking and half-ass laughing. I envisioned Squeaky walking around to Tatiana's door to open it and escort her out. He told us to get out. I grabbed Jessica's hand and we both got out of the car from my side. With Squeaky on the other side of the car helping Tatiana, me and Jessica was unguarded. We tried to hurry to the other side of the car where he was, but the mob of guys started ripping our clothes off of us. We both started screaming, scratching, and clawing to protect ourselves and hold on to each other.

"What do you think he's gonna make us do?" Tatiana asked, thankfully, interrupting my vision. It was far too vivid, beginning to cause me anxiety.

I looked at her. Her age was starting to show. That two-year difference meant a lot by the way of maturity. Or maybe she was just scared. Hoping against hope that what she felt inside was not going to be our fate. "What do you think?" I said looking away from her out of the window to grubby hands on the glass and oversized white t's.

"Oh my gosh," her voice dropped.

"We gotta get out of here."

"How? This is the first time he's left us alone since he left the hotel last night. And that was only for a few quick minutes."

"Tatiana?" I called. She just moaned. She was out of it. "I'll talk to whoever'll listen."

"If they let him walk in there with us, do you really think they'll care about what we have to say? Look at all these guys, they're all in on it...whatever *it* is."

"I'm not trying to take my clothes off, man. Not doing it."

"When we leave here, we gotta..."

"Show time, girls," he smiled opening the car door. Dread filled my heart. This was going from bad to worse. He was really about to make us get out of this car. My heart began to beat wildly. I didn't even think we'd be able to make it to the sidewalk in front of the building without our clothes being ripped off.

I opened my door and the crowd moved back a bit. I grabbed Jessica's hand and slid to get out. This was about to play out exactly as I'd envisioned. My clothes would be ripped off and the tattered shreds wouldn't cover me. This exposure was going to be much worse than just being physically naked, I'd be emotionally scarred as well.

Jessica squeezed my hand after hearing the chirp of Squeaky's car doors lock. That meant if something were to pop off, we didn't have any refuge. We couldn't scramble to get back inside. It was just us against the world. We both felt it.

We quickly walked around the car to where Squeaky was holding the door open for Tatiana. To my surprise, aside from a few ass grabs, they didn't attack us. We went inside; walked right past the bouncer without being carded or questioned. Actually, they gave Squeaky dap and ogled us right along with the rest of them.

Inside, there were small, square tables that looked like one step up from cheap card tables, and they each had two chairs at them. There were two stages and neon lights. The music was really loud, so I didn't say anything to Jessica fearing that I'd have to yell and Squeaky would hear me. As the guys trailed in behind us, Squeaky walked to the furthest corner of the room, then back again. It's like he wanted people to see us. We were on display.

There were girls on both stages and girls on the floor giving lap dances. Some were completely naked, while others were scantily clad on their way to being. Their outfits were different colors, illuminated by the black lights above head making them glow. They wore tall shoes. Really tall shoes.

We sat down and I looked around. I tried not to look at the girls in their eyes, or the patrons. I certainly was not looking over at Squeaky. I didn't want that to be like making eye contact with the teacher after they ask for volunteers to read out loud. Eye contact... *BOOM*, you're picked. I could not see myself wearing a barely there bathing suit-looking mesh outfit that didn't cover anything to begin with, only to have to take it off while dancing to a beat.

Some of the girls looked happy to be there, while others had that glazed over look Tatiana had. So, this was his plan with us all along, to put us on the stage. A waitress came over and brought a round of drinks in plastic cups. Me and Jessica shook our heads 'no', indicating we didn't want to drink. She looked at him which made us look at him. He looked at us with the stern, father face; we grabbed the cups and downed the liquor. We took it to the head. It burned.

I saw how sometimes men threw dollar bills up in the air. Those girls were standing in little piles of money. Bent over in the guys' faces, the men would run dollar bills up and down their bodies like they were playing. Other times, I saw men just hand women money folded up in his hand. I guess throwing it was more fun to them even if it ended up being the same amount. They chose to be there; we didn't.

We sat there for a few songs, during which time it was obvious that Squeaky was handling business. Guys walked up to him and spoke in his ear; sometimes he smiled a little, others he scoffed, brushing them off. The longer we sat there, the more relaxed I became. I could feel myself letting go; I didn't want to. I wanted to maintain my composure for me, Tatiana, and Jessica. The music, the darkness, the neon lights, the liquor. It calmed me in a way I did not want it to. The calmness was uncomfortable.

After he'd had enough, Squeaky stood up and pulled Tatiana up with him. He barely acknowledged me and Jessica knowing that we would be on his heels. He walked us out the long way, taking his precious time again.

That whole show at the strip club was more like a parade to show what he had. We were Squeaky's girls; his new stable of prostitutes. He was showing us off. He had to put his money where his mouth was to show them he had girls for their pleasure. Seeing so many guys at the club and at the house when we arrived made it evident that this was not his first time at the rodeo. He was used to offering girls as products and he had loyal customers who didn't care how and from where the product came. As long as it came.

I'd never felt less human in my life. I felt like a thing, like a piece of property. That's how he treated us and that's how it resonated in me. Like a scared animal that smells blood not knowing what is going to happen, but the instinctual scent lets them know it won't be good.

We pulled up to a rundown house and cars were already there. It was crawling with guys. As soon as we walked into the living room, I was whisked away down the long hall to a dark bedroom. I only got a glimpse of the wall-to-wall guys standing around the room. I heard a loud porn video, I didn't see it though. It was playing from an old, floor model TV, the kind with the big back. The room I was taken too had a huge tire in it. It was weird.

The guy pushed me down onto a mattress on the floor. On his knees, he groped my breasts with one hand while pushing my pants down with the other. At first, I resisted. The more I tried to squirm around to keep his hands from making as much contact, the more forceful he became. I knew what was coming next. There was no point to fight it. Fighting it would only be more painful for me.

I don't know how he was able to get an erection with me clearly not wanting his advances. It didn't take long for him to penetrate me. I looked at the door. I remember seeing blue lights in the house. That light seeped under the doorway. It was just a sliver of light, but I stared at it. As he pounded inside of me, I let my mind wander to the faces of my grandparents. I thought about the trips we used to take. On one trip, my family and I went to Lake Tahoe. It was so cool playing in the snow with my family. I set myself there, on the slopes in the powdery snow. At first, I was hesitant, then eager to play in it. We had so much fun. It was a much different speed for this Florida girl.

A set of shoes walked into the blue. I could see two shoes partially blocking the light coming under the doorway. There was a tap at the door. When he was done, he got up, zipped his pants which he hadn't even taken off and opened the door. He left, another guy came in. I didn't even move. I didn't give him the courtesy of looking in his face. For what? I didn't want to remember anything about him. Not the way he smelled, not the way he moved, and certainly not the way he looked. I wanted him to do his 'time' and leave me quickly.

Another pair of shoes. Same drill. A rotation. This one wanted something different. He turned me over. I just laid there. I didn't move and moan. He was gentler than the others, or maybe I was just numb.

Another pair of shoes. My mind traversed through the New Years' experience I'd just had with the girls. We had so much fun singing and laughing and talking trash. We enjoyed being around each other so much. I replayed the whole day in my head...what we did, the conversations. That seemed like a whole lifetime ago.

A lot of blue light. I heard Jessica screaming. Her screams brought me back to the present. Realizing there was nobody in the room with me, I jumped up to run out of the opened door. I ran to the mouth of the hallway where Jessica and Tatiana were standing. Jessica was no longer screaming, but she was still visibly upset. Her face was red and wet from tears that were still falling. She could not be consoled. I put my arm around my sisters.

"Naw man, I'm out." One guy said. He walked up to Squeaky with his hand out.

"C'mon nah!" Squeaky said trying to convince him not to leave. The guy looked at us, then back at Squeaky with a look that said he was not playing. He extended his hand out further and Squeaky gave him some money. Then, he had an attitude. Giving money back was not something Squeaky was used to doing. Nor did he like it.

That guy left along with a few behind him. When we tried to blend in to file out of the house with them, Squeaky stepped in to intervene. He backed us up all the way to the back room, the one I had been in. The blue light glistened on his brown skin making him look darker than he was. Shiny almost. Without saying one word, he put us in the room and closed the door.

"I can't..." Jessica began to talk. I instantly put my hand over her mouth to silence her. I pointed to the door and put my index finger over my mouth encouraging her to be quiet. I watched under the doorway until I only saw the blue light, no shoes. Then, I waited a few seconds before taking my hand down.

"That's how you can tell when somebody is outside the door," I whispered. They both nodded.

"I can't believe this is happening. If I hadn't started screaming, I'd still be in there with all those dudes," Jessica whispered back.

"All what dudes?" I asked.

"There were so many guys in that room. It's like they came out of the closet and from under the bed and from behind the door. They were everywhere," her voice dropped. Me and Tatiana looked down, sad and helpless. Sad because this was happening to us and helpless because we couldn't do anything to stop it.

"Did you see that guy give Squeaky money at the

door?" Tatiana asked.

"Yeah," I said. Jessica nodded. "He's selling us."

"Like he's our pimp? Why is he doing this?" Jessica asked rhetorically.

"I don't know. But your screaming ran them outta here."

"Maybe now, he'll let us leave."

"Then why did he put us back here?" Tatiana asked. Another rhetorical question we didn't have the answer for. There was no way of knowing what Squeaky's intentions with us were. We hadn't known anything along the way. All we knew is that he called us his girls and it didn't seem like he was willing to let us go.

TATIANA

The next morning, I woke up and we were huddled on the mattress together. *At least I'm not in it alone*, I thought. I stared up at the popcorn ceiling of the room that I didn't even remember going to. The ceiling was just like any other; however the things that happened underneath were unlike any I'd ever experienced.

I tried to recollect what happened the night before, how I got in that room. My second night with Squeaky and my second new morning waking up in a new environment. There were flashes of what happened...the cocaine...the strip club...Jessica's voice screaming. Jessica screaming. That was a little more vivid than the rest. She was so upset with me. I felt horrible. She thought I'd left her, that I'd forgotten about her. Forgot was a poor word choice. The passing of time escaped me in my disillusioned state. It's not that I wanted to sit idly by while she was being attacked, I didn't know what was going on in the room, nor was I conscious enough to pay attention to what was going on around me.

I could still hear her screams in my mind when I woke up. That sound coming from her stirred up a guilt in me that I couldn't set aside. I wondered how she was going to respond to me when she woke up, if she'd still be upset at me. She said there were so many guys taking turns that she lost count. Oh, I felt so bad for her. That could have just as easily been me in that room instead of her. There was nothing keeping me from having a rotation the night before except Squeaky wanted me by his side.

I wondered if that would be the day we were freed. I prayed that Squeaky had gotten a good night's sleep and thought about having to give money back to the guy who walked out and led other guys out with him. I prayed that would be enough to coax him to let us go.

We were all so on edge that when I sat up, Jessica and Nicole's eyes flew open. It wasn't the sleepy groggy kind of waking up where you are well rested after sleeping long and awaking naturally. It was the sudden kind of awakening, more like a jolt out of sleep, the kind that happens when someone's safety is hanging in the balance.

We all just looked at each other. I held a look with Jessica a little longer than normal. I needed to search her to see if she was still disappointed in me. The look I saw wasn't one of upset or disgust, it was a look of kindness.

I slid to the edge of the mattress.

"Where are you going?" Jessica asked.

"I gotta pee," I whispered.

"I'm going too!"

"Shoot, don't leave me in here by myself," Nicole added whispering. I opened the door slowly so it wouldn't creak waking Squeaky, or whoever else was in the house. The whoever else was in the house turned out not to be Squeaky, but his cousins. One of them bent the corner into the hallway before we made it to the bathroom.

"*Mmm hmm*," was all he said. He made eye contact with all three of us one...by one...by one. That was his way of letting us know he saw us...really *saw* us. They were watching. They were always watching.

I scampered into the bathroom with my girls right behind me. We used the bathroom, then went back into the room where we'd slept. There wasn't much in the room: a pair of tires for oversized rims, a few shoe boxes, and some clothes in the closet. After being in there for a little while, the guy from the hallway came into the room. He didn't knock, he just walked like he owned the place.

"Don't be doin' nothin' crazy in my house," he began. I guess he did own the place. "Squeaky left me here to watch y'all. But I'm not alone. So, don't think you can run over me or triple team me or no shit like that. It ain't happenin'. I got some breakfast for y'all," he said finishing with a laugh.

While we listened to his little speech, we tried

not to show our excitement at him having breakfast for us. That is, until he opened his hand and handed us all pills. Drugs for breakfast. I smacked my lips, pissed at myself for getting my hopes up at the prospect of food. It had been a while since we'd eaten. It was before we left the hotel the evening before. Then, I was pissed at him for trying it.

"Can we get some real food, man?" Jessica asked with a straight attitude. That was the Jessica I was used to seeing in school when other kids tried her. It's like she went from being scared to her old, spirited self. Being attacked the way she was the night before and learning that Squeaky was making a profit off our bodies emboldened her.

"Real food? This is the good stuff!" he smirked.

"We don't want that shit! We want real...food. We hungry, the fuck?"

He stood there taken by surprise at first, then shouted, "Shut the fuck up! Take these damn pills and I'll think about getting yo' measily ass a hamburger or some shit!" He shoved the pills at us again and we took them. He stood there to make sure we took them.

Before our food came, I guess we had to pay for

it. We were separated by force into different rooms and had to entertain guys again. It was only after that we were given food. Then, we were raped again.

Squeaky showed up to the house later that evening. He burst into the house loud and faded. "Where the fuck them girls at?" he boomed.

I didn't hear anybody say anything, so I guess they just pointed to the hallway. There were always a handful of guys in the house. Always. We could hear him coming. *Stomp. Stomp. Stomp.* His walk was hard and loud. That was different than normal. When he damn near kicked the door in, I could understand why. He was heated!

"What the hell is wrong with y'all?" he asked loud enough to hear him outside. Maybe he wanted the guys in the house to hear him checking us or he was just that upset. Above all, he was impaired. I'd never seen him that way. I'd seen him on pills, weed, and liquor; usually a combo of two out of three. He kept his system loaded up. This version of him was one he hadn't showed us.

"When my people tell you to do something, you fuckin' do it! Do you hear me?" he yelled. He'd only entered the room and I could smell the alcohol on him. "Don't have them tell me nothin' else y'all cryin' for and not doin' or not takin' or none uh dat. You," he pointed to Jessica, "you da main one. Don't be talkin' back and shit!"

"I can talk back if I want to. You don't run me!" she shouted.

"I don't..." he murmured looking left and right as if he didn't hear her correctly. He couldn't believe she responded to him that way. He had to check to make sure he heard her right. "I don't run you?"

"No! You need to just let us go!"

"I'll let you go when I get my money for you!"

"What money? You didn't spend no money on us! You didn't take us anywhere or buy us anything. You barely feed us! I want to go! We all want to go!" she shouted.

"You look like you wanna jump bad, lil' girl," he said a little softer. Me and Nicole sat on either side of her wondering which way this was going to go. Maybe this is what we had to do to get out. Be loud, boisterous.

Jessica stood up swiftly, "Let us go! I'm not one of your hoes! You can't just keep..." before she could finish, he reached over and grabbed a fist of her long, curly hair right in the middle of her head. He pulled her face close enough for her to feel the wind from his alcohol-soaked breath.

He yelled as if she was still across the room. "If you ever talk to me like that again, I'll put my sneaker so far up your ass, you'll be shitting sneaker sole for a month!"

Still in his face, Jessica screamed, "I'm not one of your hoes!"

Using his free hand to wrap it around her neck, Squeaky turned on his heels practically dragging Jessica behind him. She was kicking and screaming trying to get him off of her. I rushed after them and so did the guys who were in the house. Squeaky dragged her up the stairs to the second floor. The whole time he yanked and pulled on her, the stairs were giving her a beating as well. Her body twisted and turned as she tried to maneuver herself free.

"Let her go! Let her go!" Nicole and I shouted running behind them. He slid open a double door going from a sun room out to a balcony. When he opened the doors, I lunged at her feet and was inches away. I felt the air move as he picked her up trying to hang her over the balcony railing.

"C'mon Squeaky, man!" one of the guys yelled.

"Put the girl down, Squeaky!" said another.

"It's not that serious, let her go!" I screamed.

I lunged again, this time catching hold of her feet. She was stretched between him and me. He was pulling her; but, so was I. If he was big and bad enough to throw her over the balcony, he was going to have to be bad strong enough to fling us both over. I knew that wouldn't happen.

There was so much happening at once. Pure chaos. She was screaming and crying by that point. Squeaky was yelling. His friends and cousins were trying to talk him down. I was screaming and crying. Nicole appeared to be in shock. After several minutes of him taunting her, the guys wrangled her from his grasp. I don't think he would've dropped her, but at that moment, it would have been hard to convince her otherwise.

As soon as her body hit the ground, she jumped up and snatched a beer bottle from the corner of the balcony. She launched that thing at Squeaky while screaming like a madwoman. He tried to jump back at her, but the other guys tussled with him until they pushed him back in the house.

They didn't bother fooling with us. Not right away, at least. They knew we weren't going to jump off the balcony. We were so busy trying to wrap our heads around what had just happened, jumping off the balcony into freedom hadn't even crossed our minds.

Jessica's face was red from crying and yelling and fighting.

"Y'all just gonna let him kill me?! Why did y'all let him do that me? Hang me over the damn balcony?" she crumbled into a ball of tears. She slid down the railing onto the balcony, put her head into her hands and cried.

"What was I supposed to do?" I asked in frustration. "I was right there pulling on you trying to get you away from him!"

"I don't know!" she yelled. "Something!"

"I was doing *something*! This is not normal! This isn't something we're supposed to even be going through! Like, what the hell?"

"You could've jumped on his ass, damn!"

"How Jessica? He was against the railing and all

those guys were up here! They are men, Jessica, grown ass men. They are bigger and stronger than we are. Even the three of us all together."

Nicole sat next to her and embraced her. Jessica sobbed. Loud sounds of a young girl who'd been through so much unimaginable anguish over the last 48 hours. She was hungry, frustrated, tired of being used, weary from being drugged. I was all those things and then some. So was Nicole.

thirteen

NICOLE

My heart broke seeing Jessica so...shattered. It seemed like he went from yelling at her to hanging her over the balcony in a matter of seconds. It was so scary. Him yelling; her standing up for herself, for us. That was the Jessica I'd heard about. I knew she was no stranger to fighting. I definitely wasn't a fighter. There were four of us in that room. The three of us could have taken Squeaky. If it were just the three of us. There were so many other people in that house. Because we were ostracized to the room, there was no way of knowing exactly how many men were in the house, but there were two things for sure. One, we were outnumbered. And two, we were out sized; they were grown men.

I sat next to her on the balcony and rubbed her head as she cried. She was so mad. It seemed like she directed more rage to Tatiana than to Squeaky. Jessica had to calm down. Tatiana leaned on the railing, searching herself to see if she'd really done all she could. Watching the whole thing, I knew she had.

I was more concerned with how that interaction was going to impact us moving forward. What did that mean for us? Were they going to drug us? Were they going to tie us up? Were they going to let us go? A neighbor could have easily heard and/or seen the spectacle Squeaky put on that balcony. I was hopeful that he would realize we weren't worth the trouble of him keeping us.

Instead, he drugged us up even more that night. After one of his do boys gave us a hand of pills and big cups of Hennessy, I don't remember anything until the next day. I do remember looking at all of the pills they made us take thinking, *I have to do something to get us out of here!* They had never given us that many pills. I guess it was to make us pay for what had happened with Jessica earlier.

The next few days were more of the same. Barely any food, handfuls of pills, cups of Hennessy, and a constant barrage of men. The house had a weird smell to me. Maybe it was a mix of the weed they smoked and having lots of many different men with their weed and alcohol laden breath laughing and talking loud, in and out of the house. It reeked. The stench never went away and I never forgot it.

Keeping us loaded allowed leeway for our captors to let down their guards. I found a cell phone. I knew exactly what to do with it. I called my mother. She didn't answer. So, I called the next best option, my boyfriend.

"Baby, it's me," I whispered.

"Nicole!" he shouted. "Where the hell are you? I've been looking everywhere for you. We've been looking everywhere for you. How are you? Are you ok?"

"No, no. I'm not ok. I was kidnapped."

"Where are you?"

"I don't know."

"Man, we've been putting up missing posters

with your picture!" he started to cry. "We've been looking everywhere."

"They have us! They're holding us. Me, Tatiana, and Jessica," I whispered.

"Where are you? What do you see around you?"

"Hold on," I said. I repositioned myself in a room on the front side so I could see out of the window. "I just see a bunch of trees."

"No street signs?"

"No. A dumpster."

"Did you call your mom?"

"Yeah, she didn't answer. You gotta come get us. Send help," I pleaded.

"I need to know where you are. Try to find a landmark or street sign or something! We can't find you if we don't know where you are. Let me try your mom on three-way."

While he tried to get her on the line, I snuck out of the house. I was desperate to find something, anything that would help me tell them where I was. Once clear of the house, I cautiously ran across the grass to get to the street.

"Nicole!" my mother's voice came on the line.

"Mom!" I said exasperated. For the first time, hearing my mother's voice brought happy tears to my eyes. This was it. This was how I could get me and the girls out of this hell we'd been living for a week.

"Where are you? Are you ok?"

"All I see are trees and houses. Nothing else. I'm trying to find a street sign."

No sooner than those words crossed my lips, Squeaky came barreling across the grass towards me in his car. Instead of slowing down to park, he sped up when he saw me. Even with the sun's reflection on the glass, my eyes met his. His were full of rage.

"NO! NO! NO!" I screamed, still holding the phone to my ear.

"What's happening?"

"Nicole! Nicole! Talk to us!"

My mother and boyfriend went crazy hearing me scream. I can only imagine what they envisioned. Before the car came to a stop, Squeaky hopped out and was seemingly running alongside it. I dropped the phone and tried to run. He came behind me, snatched me by my hair and drug me inside the house the same way he drug Jessica.

fourteen
TATIANA

    I heard a commotion from outside. Whatever it was, it wasn't good. A car's engine revved and the body squeaked as the suspension bounced on the uneven grass in the yard. Then, I heard Squeaky and Nicole yelling. Maybe Nicole starting yelling first. He ended it though. I could tell that he was trying to stifle her while disciplining her at the same time.

    I could only envision what was happening. Me and Jessica tried to run to the door, but we were stopped by one of Squeaky's do boys. Nicole's screaming got louder and louder, then *BOOM*...Squeaky damn near kicked the door in dragging her into the house. She was kicking and screaming while he told her to, "Shut the fuck up, bitch!"

Squeaky turned to his boys, "How did she get out of the house? And how did she get hold to a phone?!" he yelled at them breathlessly, tired from fighting a girl almost his same size. "If you don't want to watch 'em, get the hell outta here, mane! I pull up and see her ass outside!"

Phone? Nicole had a phone? Even though the moment had passed, I was still a little excited that she managed to get her hands on a phone. There was a glimmer of hope. They were slipping up.

Surely, she knew who to call. I hoped a search party was forming or cops were on the way with helicopters, lights and sirens. Something. Anything. Just like on TV, the good guys would come swooping in to save us. I expected grand heroism! I just wanted to be free; we just wanted to be free.

"Y'all little heffas gettin' real spicy. I got somethin' for that ass." Hearing those words, my eyes slammed shut. I knew what that meant. It was either going to be more men or more drugs. Neither was a door we would have chosen. It was going to be all bad.

Squeaky took a handful of pills and shoved them in Nicole's mouth. Jessica and I were next. A dry, crusty, ashy Squeaky's handful of pills. We washed them down with brown liquor. Looking back, it's a wonder we didn't die during the time he had us. Clearly, he didn't care what happened to us and we were not in a position to take care for ourselves. At certain points, I felt like we could die and he would step over our decaying corpses and walk out the door.

I was so proud of my girl for trying to get us out of the situation, but it really put us in a worse predicament. Now, instead of them slipping up on us, they would be hawking our every move. Us almost getting out was going to cause our gatekeepers hell to pay. If the police didn't get there first. They didn't want Squeaky being upset with them. I knew he was going to keep us drugged for real now. He was not going to slip up on us. If he let anybody else watch us, they were going to have to be on it! It didn't seem like he was going to leave anybody else up to the task.

As he shouted at us about what not to do and

how not to act, the fading flooded in. We were fed pills more than food. On an empty stomach and being barely 110 pounds, the drugs were going to have their way with me and there was nothing I could do about it. I could barely pay attention to what he was saying, much less be cognizant enough to nod acknowledging that I heard him and was listening.

Fading...fading...fading...I was in my room laying on my bed. I looked around and saw everything just as I'd left it. Everything was in its place. Not common for me, or many kids my age. I cleaned my room so my mom wouldn't have anything to say about me hanging out with Nicole and Jessica at the mall. I had plans to be gone most of the day, not a week. *Ugh!* The mall...that day...I didn't want to think about that.

I directed my thoughts back to being in my room. I was sitting Indian style on my bed. Looking down, two of my dolls appeared in my hands. I played with them. Yes, even at 12, I still played with dolls. I would have never admitted that to the girls. Play with dolls? Who me? Naw. Then I got up and looked at myself in the mirror. I turned to the left and right to look at myself. Nothing about me looked hardened or mature. I wasn't fast. Maybe that's what the guys saw when they looked at me. My innocence. I played in my hair, styling it this way and that. Then I tried on a few different outfits. I killed Rocawear; I had jean shorts and skirts, and regular jeans in just about every color they came in. Couldn't tell me nothing. My favorite outfit was a burgundy jean skirt with a pink shirt. I threw on some Reeboks and was ready to go! I was fly!

I could hear my mother and little brother playing in the living room. Since she was a single mother, there wasn't much time for this kind of leisurely playing. In my state, I needed as much positivity as I could get if I was going to survive. My brother's laugh was so infectious. He was so bubbly and so innocent, when he wasn't being a whirlwind of dirty clothes, messy eating, and leaving his G.I. Joes and race cars all over the house.

I cracked my room door open to see them. They were just as chipper. My mother's face was beautiful, free of worry. A smile came to my lips seeing her face. That was all I needed to feel a sense of home, my mother's face. I rushed over to her and she stood up to hug me. She tried to let go, but I wouldn't. I held her, listening to the sound of her heartbeat. Home.

The thing about being high was I could lucid dream. In lucid dreams, I was still asleep and dreaming, however I had control of my dreams. When my thoughts took me down a road I didn't want to go down, like thinking about the day Squeaky picked us up or being at the hotel, or any of the events that happened at the house, I could push those thoughts to the side, rerouting my ideas to something more pleasant.

When I came to, I was shivering. Hungry and cold. Famished even. We almost never had on clothes. He did it for two reasons: so we couldn't hide anything and to deter us from leaving. Concealing a cell phone would be impossible, even if we could get our hands on one. Running out the door butt naked would make me think twice about running if I got the chance. At 12, I didn't want to be seen in my birthday suit. Not to mention the moist air making the chilly January seem even colder. Streaking in January was not the move for us as teens. Perhaps if we were more accustomed to the street life; but, we weren't.

The drugs and nakedness were his ways of keeping us in order. They worked. We all fought back at times, but it got to the point of relenting. What were we fighting for? He was not going to let us go until he was good and ready. There was only so much we could do.

Usually, they kept us in the back room with the big tires when we weren't being prostituted out. Huddled together on the bed, there wasn't much to talk about. We all shared the same sentiments. We'd been together from the beginning of this hellacious ordeal, we knew what was happening. Although not completely.

We didn't talk about what was happening to us when we were separated away from each other, alone in the rooms with the guys. When we were chosen. Talking about it would have been like reliving it. There was no need to breathe life into the constant rapes we were enduring multiple times a day, day after day. There was no screaming, there was no crying. At a certain point, we just moved like cattle; herded to wherever he wanted us to go. We didn't want to be combative, that would have been a harder time for us.

Squeaky opened the bedroom door. He stepped to the side and in stepped another customer. We all tried to look away. We each looked so similar, it didn't really matter. He must've pointed at me. Squeaky walked over and nudged my shoulder. Letting out an exasperated exhale, I got up from the tattered mattress on the floor. I was up. Still coming down from my high, I dragged my feet as I followed behind my first customer of the day. He certainly wouldn't be my last. There was no telling how many customers I'd seen in a day. I lost count. One...one hundred; they were all the same.

He did his business on me, unwanted, like Mister in *The Color Purple*. When he was finished, he got up and left the room. I guess he got what he came for because he wasn't upset or fussing when he left. Nor did Squeaky come blasting back in the room because I'd done something 'wrong.' Nevermind his whole operation being wrong.

There were times when Squeaky yelled at me for walking to the room too slowly or acting like I had an attitude. He strong armed me to get me in the room faster and at night, rarely turned the lights on. There was mostly a light illuminating from the hallway. The customers could barely see what they were getting. Clearly, they weren't the discerning type. He'd yell because I didn't throw it back like he taught me or yell because I was in the bathroom too much. He could check me while selling my body. But he kept right on doing it.

I waited for a while to see if he was going to come rushing back into the room threatening to hit me again or shoving my breakfast pills down my throat. When he did neither, I walked back to the room with Jessica and Nicole. I ran my hands along the dirty, pastel paint. The house had not been taken care of. It looked and smelled like a bunch of nasty dudes were living there. The carpet had become crunchy, the furniture had all but fallen apart. The smell...the smell...the smell...there was a heavy, hanging stench in the air.

The walk down the hallway always seemed to take forever. Probably because I was always impaired. Or perhaps it was because I was going further into a dungeon of loathing. The comfort was safety in numbers. As long as we were together, there was a comfort. If I had to be stuck in hell, at least I was there with people I loved. I wasn't all alone. The three of us were together. We would not leave each other. Squeaky knew it; so did each of us. This experience fortified our sisterhood.

NICOLE

This fool tried to run me over with a car. Like, had the audacity to try to run me over. Days later, I was still fixated on it. At 13 years old, I'd had the first attempt on my life. And for what? Trying to get back home to my mom? The sound of my boyfriend breaking down also kept running through my mind. It was puppy love, but in my heart and mind, I knew he loved me.

If I'd had just one more minute to talk to them. One more minute to run up the street. One identifying street sign or building. We could have gotten free. Sixty more seconds was the difference in giving my mom and boyfriend the information they needed to send help. Either they would have come or sent the police. Either way, the shackles would have been loosed.

The days all ran together. It was hard to keep track of the sunrises and sunsets being heavily drugged and liquored up. Most of the windows had blinds drawn with thick, heavy window treatments. It always felt like nighttime. Actually, going outside trying to sneak on the phone was the first time I'd seen or felt the sun in a week. At the time, I had such a one-track mind I didn't think about being outside in that way. My mind was on one thing and one thing only...freedom.

I looked over at my sisters. They were starting to look different. Tired. They were getting dark circles under their eyes. I guess I must have had them, too. Something had to give. My mother wasn't big on religion. She didn't have much time for that between rotating boyfriends in and out of our lives. I knew there was a higher power despite having not spent significant amounts of time doing any of the spiritual stuff like reading my bible or praying or going to church. I prayed to God to save us. It was the only thing I knew to do.

We'd fought back. We'd protested. We'd refused. We'd tried to get away. I had no intention on being a sex slave for the rest of my life.

All three of us were tired. Words cannot express how emotionally, physically, and psychologically drained we were. At 12 and 13, we weren't that spirited. The little bit we had was leaving us. Partially from being under substance control and partially from knowing no good was going to come from us fighting them. We'd bucked the system enough; the result was still the same.

With everything running together, it was hard to recall anything. I didn't want to remember anything that had happened. When we escaped, whenever that was, I wanted to pick up with my life from leaving the mall. I didn't want to relive anything else that had happened. When the guys pounded on top of me, I often turned to the side and tried to imagine anything else I could have been doing and anywhere else I could have been. I didn't want to smell their foul breath or musky body odor. I didn't want to hear the sounds they made when pleasuring themselves on top of me.

I prayed again. I prayed that I would be able to leave this behind me. I wanted to walk out and be washed clean from the countless men who turned my body into a playground. When I wasn't playing, I thought of 572 ways to kill Squeaky. The whole house could blow up leaving no trace of him for all I cared. He didn't deserve the very air his lungs used. I felt myself growing colder inside. This was not the way for a pretty, young girl to be.

After holding us captive for God knew how long, I guess one of the do boys finally summoned an ounce of pity for us. He didn't say anything with his words, there was no need for that. It was his actions that did the talking. He walked in the room and threw our crumpled up clothes on the ground. At first, we just stared at him, almost needing instructions. He looked at us with stretched eyes like, 'You know what to do.' Then he walked over to the backdoor, opened it, then walked away.

Frozen, we sat there. It took all of five milliseconds before we jumped at the opportunity to smell our freedom before he changed his mind or somebody else changed it for him. We each threw on our clothes and ran out of the door.

It was very dramatic. We ran, I mean bolted out

of the door and down the street. We ran like track stars only to get to the intersection and realize we knew where we were. We were only a few streets over from Jessica's house. I don't think any of us looked back. I didn't. Not one single time. Forward was the only place I wanted to go...and fast.

TATIANA

The sun on my face. The wind in my hair. The chill on my arms. The convergence of these three sensations meant one thing: freedom. The feeling of my feet pounding that asphalt running for my life fueled a surge of adrenaline in my body. Fight-or-flight. I wasn't fighting. The only option was to flight. Flee. Run. Run from the scene of the crime. Crimes that were acted against me and my sisters. We could have gotten track medals for our speed.

"This way," Jessica said breathlessly as we

reached the end of the street. She didn't hesitate or stutter. She turned the corner and we followed right behind her. She seemed to increase speed the further away we got from the house, so we had to do the same to keep up. I wanted to look behind me; I knew better than that. Looking back would only slow me down. I couldn't afford that. I needed to be as far away from Squeaky and his do boys as I possibly could. *Oh my gosh! We gotta hurry up! We have to get as far away from that house as possible. What the hell? C'mon Tatiana, c'mon girl! Keep running. FASTER!*

I couldn't shake the thought that Squeaky was going to bust around the corner and we would be toast. I didn't even want to imagine the look on his face if he saw us fleeing for our lives. The disappointed father. How would he react if he caught us? He'd probably kill us on sight. We knew too much and had seen so many.

I heard loud bass pumping from a car. The car was moving quickly because I heard the sound moving. "Hide!" I screamed. We all ducked behind a wide tree. The shrubs around it were overgrown, making it wide enough to conceal our three, tiny teen bodies. As fast as we'd been sprinting, it was hard steadying our breath.

The car was flying up the street. The roar from the engine made our beating hearts pound even faster. I squeezed my eyes tight. "Lord, please don't let Squeaky see us," I murmured. I was convinced it was Squeaky and he was on his way back to the house.

The first thing he would do was check on his girls. He'd come in the house, walk down the hallway, then start singing, "London bridges falling down, my... fair... ladies..." By the time he got to 'ladies', he was at the door of the back bedroom. Little did I know, even though I never had to hear his rendition of the song ever again, he'd ruined it for me for the rest of my life. I'd never be able to hear the lullaby without feeling a guttural cringe in the pit of my stomach.

Once the car passed us, Jessica took off. She wasn't about to leave us behind, we took off, too. I knew where I was. It looked vaguely familiar. We were streets away from where Jessica lived with her grandparents. All that time, we'd been a rock's throw away from safety. Seeing familiar surroundings brought a feeling of exuberance. We were free! I started crying as we took those last few strides.

"NANA! PAPA! NANA OPEN THE DOOR!" Jessica

screamed at the top of her lungs. It was a wonder she had enough breath to run and yell at the same time. But, there's a difference when you are running and yelling for your very existence. Our lives had been hanging in the balance long enough. This was the pot of gold at the end of the rainbow. We all began yelling.

"NANA! PAPA! OPEN THE DOOR!" Jessica's grandmother, Nana, opened the door with a look of bewilderment on her face. I can only imagine how she felt seeing the three of us running toward her. Wild and crazy, arms flailing, yelling loud enough to wake the dead. Jessica, who was still in the front, leaned forward like she was going to break the tape at a track meet. She ran into her grandmother's arms so hard, she pushed her back into the trailer door.

I got inside and slammed the door closed, then frantically locked it. Nana and Jessica were on the floor clutching each other, crying loudly. Nana kept pulling Jessica back to look at her face, then pulling her back down for a hug, crying the whole time. Papa, Jessica's grandfather, hugged me and Nicole. We were so relieved. It felt so good to be around people we knew we were safe to be with. We collapsed into his embrace as he wiped a tear from his eye.

"Go to your Papa," Nana said to Jessica who turned around and saw us standing with him. She stood up and we stepped to the side so she could have a moment with him. Nana opened her arms to me and Nicole, then we hugged her also. More tears, happy tears. The emotional reunion seemed to last forever. I didn't mind. I'd much rather have been standing in Nana and Papa's trailer crying, than lying in the back bedroom with the huge tires squeezing my eyes so tightly tears fell in my effort to forget where I was and what was happening to me.

"Nana, may I call my mom?" I asked.

"Oh yes, baby! Yes, yes! You didn't even have to ask!" she said moving quickly to hand me their house phone. Just as quickly as she moved, she was standing right back in place on the other side of Jessica. "What happened? Where were you? Why were you gone so long? I...we were so worried about you!" Nana began crying all over again.

As more tears spilled onto her cheeks on top of wet stains that hadn't been wiped away or dried yet, I eagerly dialed my mom's number. "Hello?" she answered. Hearing her voice sent shockwaves through my body. My eyes brimmed with tears while I struggled to get the words out of my open mouth. "Hello?" she asked again, this time sounding a little more pissed. I'm sure she thought it was somebody playing on her phone.

"Mom," breathlessly. At last, a word.

"Tati? Tati! TATIANA!! Oh my gosh, Tatiana! Baby! How are you?"

"Mom! MOM!"

"Where are you? Are you ok? I'm coming, where are you?" I handed Nana the phone and she told my mom how to get to her house. Nicole followed suit, calling her mother to come get her.

I'm not sure relief is a grand enough word to describe how I felt being out of that dungeon and in Nana and Papa's house. My mom was on the way. Within the next 20 minutes, she'd be standing in front of me, hugging and kissing me. I could not wait. What tween wants to be lavished with kisses from their mother? This girl. I could not wait to see her with my own eyes. A part of me still felt that Squeaky was going to appear, beating the door down to take us back by force. It wouldn't be tough to overpower Jessica's grandparents. They were older and, obviously, not as strong as Squeaky and his crew. Nor did they have guns to scare Squeaky with, that I knew of.

The chances' of Squeaky popping up commandeering us were slim-to-none, but you couldn't tell my heart and mind that. I was convinced this feeling of finally being free was one he could take away from us in a fleeting moment. I would die if I had to be in his grasp again.

While we waited on our mothers to come, we went to the bathroom to shower. Showering wasn't high on Squeaky's list of things for us to do. It didn't require a penis, drugs, or alcohol, and surely wasn't making him any money. Being as young as we were, it wasn't exactly a high priority for us either. Sure, we were used to taking showers before bed or in the morning before going to school as a part of our normal routine. What had been normal or routine about what we had going on? Not to mention he kept us so high we didn't even know what time of day it was or how many days had passed since our last shower. We weren't clothed, so we weren't stinking up our clothes to know we needed a shower. For Squeaky and his customers, it was all about easy access. They wanted us when they wanted us how they wanted us.

Maybe it was because of our friendship bond that grew during our being held hostage or perhaps it was because for the last month we'd stayed together as a means of comfort and protection, but when one moved, all moved. The three of us went into the bathroom together, eager to wash the experience away. If only it was as easy as water, soap, lather, rinse, and dry.

The warm water felt so good on my skin. For the first time in a long time, we were able to take an uninterrupted shower. There was no threat of Squeaky or his goons bursting through the door. We didn't have to worry about being dragged from the shower, dripping wet, into the bedroom and tossed onto the soiled mattresses on the floor. There was no concern of us slipping and falling on the floor being yelled at to hurry so he could make his money off our bodies.

Honestly, I didn't want to get out. I was so at peace standing under the cascading drops of water, ridding my body and my mind of trauma. I'd take any morsel of peace and comfort I could get at that point.

Even knowing we were safe, we still remained

together. The three of us stayed in the bathroom together. Showered together. "Who's bleeding?" Jessica asked. We all looked down. Checking ourselves and each other.

"Tatiana! You're bleeding," Nicole said. She wasn't upset or alarmed, just matter-of-fact. We realized that after the most harrowing ordeal of our lives, I'd just started my period.

Nana ran into the bathroom, "You can't shower! You can't shower! You're washing evidence down the drain!" We jumped out as quickly as we could. The calm, relaxing shower ended up not being so calm and relaxing after all. "Pat dry," she instructed and we did just that.

Not so long after, the police arrived. Them showing up to Nana and Papa's was not exactly the way I'd envisioned the scenario with them replaying in my head day in and day out countless times. I wanted the police to use a ram to knock down the door to Squeaky's brothel shouting at all of the guys to put their hands up. I wanted the place to be full of customers lining the wall, so they all could go to jail. I wanted it loud and messy, where their faces were splattered across the news and me and my sisters were rescued like the damsels in distress we were.

Instead of my grand daydream, one of our gatekeepers just opened the back door and let us out. Something he could have done long before. Nevertheless, I was grateful for the conscience he gained even if it came after unconscionable damage had been done. We'd survived.

"So, your grandma here tells me you girls were kidnapped?" the officer asked almost in disbelief.

"Yes," we bashfully admitted.

He looked at us and squinted his eyes. He looked us over from head-to-toe for traces of physical abuse, of which there weren't any. By that point, Squeaky had us marching a straight line, so we knew better than to act out. We danced to the beat of his drum. Jessica and Nicole had already suffered his wrath being beaten and hung over the balcony. "Kidnapped."

"Yes," I said. "They gave us drugs and liquor and paid him to have sex with us."

"Paid him, who?"

"Squeaky," Jessica blurted. "Our kidnapper's name is Squeaky."

"So, you know your 'kidnapper'?" he asked skeptically saying 'kidnapper' like he clearly doubted our truth.

"No, he took us off the street, we were walking home. We heard the guys call him by his name."

"What's his real name?"

"We don't know! We don't know him!" Jessica got upset. She could tell he did not believe her.

"Why don't we start from the beginning," he offered sensing her irritability and wanting to calm her down.

"We were walking here from the bus stop..." I began and told the story. Places where I spaced out, Jessica and Nicole jumped in to fill in the blanks. Keeping us high was a good strategy on Squeaky's part, our memories were so foggy. I'm sure we sounded crazy to them all, especially the officer who didn't know us from cans of paint.

By the time we were finished, he had no choice but to believe our story. We were consistent, animated, and passionate. At a time, I even cried while describing some of the things that had been done to us. Our parents were there listening. I saw the horror on my mother's face hearing about how her oldest child was defiled of my virginity. Nana kept rubbing Jessica's back, especially when she unsuccessfully held back the tears when recounting her balcony fight with Squeaky.

The officer knew what he had to do; the next steps were obvious. All we had was a street name and didn't know exactly where we'd been, but could probably retrace our freedom flight if necessary.

"We're gonna take you girls to a hospital to perform a rape kit on you," the officer said.

"Well, they just got out of the shower," Nana admitted. "We didn't have all the details, well, as many as you do right now. And we were so overwhelmed seeing the girls for the first time in a month. I wasn't paying attention when they turned on the shower."

A month? Did Nana just say we'd been gone for a month? A whole 30 days? Wow! Not only had I lost my innocence, sense of security and comfort, I'd also lost so much time out of my life. I was sure it had been more than a week, but a month? I wasn't anticipating that.

"Ugh," he said let down. We'll do the best we can. Since you've showered, that's precious evidence we can't recover. Hopefully, the rape kit will point us in the right direction."

We didn't know what a rape kit was, but we soon found out. Probably because of the desperately needed shower we took before they arrived, they had to do an invasive kit. Like Nana said, we'd washed away evidence. Our bodies had to be laden with DNA from Lord knows how many offenders. The names of the men who'd paid to rape us washed down the drain along with the stench of their bodies we wanted to scrub ourselves clean of.

A lot of the memories immediately following are hazy due to us coming down off of the drugs and being so bombarded with emotions and describing recollections. I do remember lying on a table with a bright light on top of me. My mother was just to my side, holding my hand letting me know it was ok and I was safe.

There was a big TV on the wall. I could see inside myself. I remember the lady putting something inside of me, then seeing inside of my vagina on the TV. That is an image I'll never forget.

seventeen

NICOLE

My mom got to Nana and Papa's house before Tatiana's mom. I'd already cried a few times that day, which was really out of character for me. Mostly once we got to the trailer and I saw Nana standing in the doorway. It was like, 'Yes! Finally!' Such a wave of consolation flushed over me.

Seeing my mother was something different. Hugging Nana and Papa in the safety of their home was cool and all. They were Jessica's grandparents, not mine. I'd only known Jessica a little while before all of this happened. I hadn't had the opportunity to interact with them besides when they answered the phone and I asked to speak to Jessica. So, viewing them as responsible adults who I knew would not hurt me was good; but, not nearly as comforting as seeing my own mother.

We weren't exactly the emotional or touchy-feely type of family, nor were we particularly close. There was no way I could look at her and give her a regular hug after not seeing her face for God knows how long. We still had no idea how long we'd been gone. I wrapped my arms around her and didn't want to let to go. Seeing her, holding her, smelling her. Like a newborn baby who identifies their mother by her distinct smell, I inhaled her scent into my nostrils. Deep inhale and exhale, inhale and exhale, deeper, deeper...tears. I tried to keep it together. How could I after everything?

The days that followed were a mess. We had been so high for so long, my body had a hard time adjusting to not getting Squeaky's usual diet... a handful of pills for breakfast, a handful of pills for dinner, and brown liquor to wash it all down and in between. Going cold turkey off any substance is hard. Operating almost solely on drugs and alcohol was initially a shock to our systems. Somehow we'd survived and even got used to it. Our bodies got used to the intake and we got used to the feeling. Coming down from the use was equally as challenging, probably moreso.

We were ordered into a drug rehab facility to be weaned off our recent introduction. It was a lockdown facility, very sterile, very scary. Of course at that age, I didn't know what to expect. "This is going to help get those drugs out of your system and get you back to normal," we were told. What wasn't explained to us was that we were essentially going from one form of imprisonment to another, except at this one, we were far from the guests of honor. We were shoved into rooms while other patients who had strong, long-term addictions and others with mental disorders, including schizophrenia, took precedence.

I couldn't be free and still not be free. Being there was not therapy, it was a babysitter service to keep us tied down from getting drugs, as if we took them voluntarily. *Slap!* I jumped at the sound of the big, metal doors slamming shut. Over and over, several times a day. Every time I heard that sound, it was like Squeaky was coming back to the house. That door sound meant more customers he wanted us to service.

On top of the monochromatic color scheme and tasteless food, my body was going through withdrawals. I had used my grandparents' house as a mental escape for so long, that could not give me enough calmness to focus on the benefit of staying at the facility. So many strangers, doctors and nurses coming and going. They looked at me like I'd done something wrong; it seemed they stared at me as one of the youngest people in the building. Their stares almost whispered to me, *Look at that fast little girl. Didn't she know better? Thirteen and already addicted to drugs. What a damn shame. Giving her parents such a hard time. She needs to be in school.*

In my mind, I cried in response. *No! It wasn't my fault. I didn't do anything wrong! They did it to me! To us! Help me!*

None of them seemed to care enough to genuinely try to help me. They came to the hospital putting in their eight hour shifts so they could collect a check. Instead of being helped, it seemed we only received hefty servings of judgement.

My soul craved peace. I couldn't stand it. I needed to be in a familiar environment that was safe. I got the hell out of dodge as fast as I could. I ran back to the closest place I knew could find security.

I'm not quite sure what type of reaction my mom was waiting on. As the days went by, she got angry with me like the whole situation was my fault. She treated me like I ran away, like I wanted to be gone. She thought I ran away to be fast, to be with boys, and doing drugs was my choice. I was not that girl. I wasn't the type to get in trouble at school. Sure, I talked back occasionally, but skipping school and using was not my M.O.

After running away from the drug rehab back to my mom's, she rushed me back into my regular routine. She was dead set on moving on as if nothing happened. She did what she thought was in her best interest, not mine. There are two routes to take when someone has been through an emotional experience: take time to heal and recover or dive headfirst back into the thick of it. The latter is what my mother chose. The thought of getting me back into a routine offered a sense of normalcy; however, after enduring something so horrific, I needed time to heal.

There was a huge divide going from being high 24/7 and prostituted out to multiple men throughout the day to waking up to an alarm to catch the bus for middle school and chatting with the girls about nail polish colors and who liked who.

I found myself still wanting to be numb. Numb not to remember, numb not to think about it, numb not to be so jumpy, numb to function. I'd sneak into my mother's medicine cabinet to get my hands on whatever I could. I didn't really know what I was doing, but I knew the more pills Squeaky gave me, the more numb I became. Memories weren't as vivid as they normally would have been, the pain didn't hurt as much, the smell of the men and the house wasn't as loud. None of it went away, it was just more dull than it could have been. What I craved was the dullness.

There was no discernment in my selection. If it was going to alter my mental state in any way, I took it. After all, I'd survived ecstasy, heroin, and coke, sometimes mixed together. Surely, I could survive what was in my mother's medicine cabinet. Was I even trying to survive? Did I want to be alive, bound to the hauntingly frightful events we'd experienced? How was

I supposed to move forward in life when I couldn't erase the most recent chapter and no one was counseling me through it? How did my mother expect me to go cold turkey off drugs after a few days in rehab, then jump back into a normal 13 year old life?

The more thoughts about my existence came to mind, the less I wanted to... exist. As much as I wanted to believe my mother missed me and was looking for me while being held hostage, getting back to her didn't give me the same vibes. It didn't seem like she missed me as much as I thought she would or cared what happened to me after. She hurled insults at me which, again made me question my existence. Cough syrup, down the hatch. Another bottle, gone in a few seconds. One day, I took an entire bottle of aspirin hoping to numb myself to death. At least that way, I wouldn't have to feel anymore. Nor did I think my mother would miss me.

Death didn't find me, but numbness did. When I went to school, I was completely zoned out. I was a walking medicine cabinet. My mother never addressed the missing pills or empty bottles in the trash. She didn't ask how I was feeling or notice my zombie-like state.

There was no urgency to care for Nicole.

The school noticed though. I'd take whatever pills I could get my hands on, Tylenol, aspirin, Benadryl, and wash them down with whatever cough syrup I could find; just the way Squeaky taught me. The taste was gross; I'd grown accustomed to it. What was important was getting to the feeling they gave me. I had to get to the goal of being numb, dull, #unbothered.

I carried my stash with me to school in my bookbag and medicated myself as needed during the day. My mother didn't notice I was a shell of myself; yet, she was keen on punishing me when I got suspended for drugging myself in the middle school bathrooms.

Punishment after punishment after punishment. That was her way of dealing with me being 'bad' and 'disobedient'. At no point did she stop to think this was a cry for help, even if my cry was subconscious. 'What is wrong? How can I help? What do you need from me? Do you want to talk to someone?' Those were not questions she asked me.

Eventually, dangerous school behaviors led to her putting me into a group home for defiant girls. How, at 13, was she kicking me out of my house? Instead of trying to get to the root of the problem, she gave up on me. Imagine that feeling of helplessness and self-hatred I felt during such a critical point in my life. She gave up on me after I was old enough to know her, remember her, and have a normal life. Not that we were so close before, but I was not an infant or a child who was too young to understand what was going on.

My mother drove me to the group home and dropped me off. Just like that. There was no conversation about her being fed up or this being in my best interest. It felt more like a sneaky operation which, to her credit, was how she'd been doing things. The right hand never knew what the left hand was doing. One day, she just dropped me off.

Why is my mom doing this to me? Why is she not trying to help me? Why is she betraying me? Betrayal. I felt like I was crying out for help, but from my lens, she kept making herself the victim. When talking about what was going on to friends and family she'd say, "Why is Nicole doing this to me?" Somehow everything that happened to me, I was doing to her.

My mom's focus was on her failed marriage's winding road through divorce and keeping her bed smoking hot with the next guy. While she was on to the next, I was stuck on the last...the last memory, last struggle, last feeling of 'home' I could remember feeling. Every time I called her, she was in a different place. Vegas, Texas, and Cali. She lived on a plane traveling to this place and that, meeting new guys at every turn. Meanwhile, I was straining to make it in the group home. I ran away.

Bouncing back and forth between juvenile halls, group homes, and my mom's, nothing was comfortable for me anymore. I didn't feel safe or understood.

TATIANA

Home didn't feel like home for me anymore. The ordeal was only a few weeks, but it felt like a few months. Each day felt like several in our dazed state. The drugs kept us confused and less combative. We couldn't tell how many days were moving on the calendar. When lucid, which was few and far between, we were jumpy, clingy, and terrified.

It lasted long enough for me to accept that we would never be found or have the opportunity to escape. If one of us did escape, whoever remained behind would be severely retaliated against or worse, killed. The combination of going to the first club where Squeaky paraded us around, seeing the guys completely surround the car and us transitioning to the house and seeing so many men I couldn't even count dashed my hopes of getting out of there. If so many guys saw us and, I'm sure could tell we were drugged when they were raping us without caring, how were we going to get out of it?

The drugs probably helped to encourage my lackluster attitude of acceptance into my fate. I couldn't even think long-term about what the future held. For the foreseeable days, weeks, and months ahead, I was going to be a prisoner under Squeaky's thumb. There was no hope of going back to my regular teenage life.

However, when we were given the opportunity to get the hell on, it only took a few seconds for us to snatch that chance and, literally, run with it! Once I overcame the fear that Squeaky would see us and shoot us dead in the street or force us back into his lair, my heart was filled with the enthusiasm of going back home.

By that time, going home had such a more heartfelt meaning. Going home meant being in familiar surroundings, being around people I loved who knew me and cared for me. It meant feeling safe and secure. It meant taking showers by myself, not worried about whether a stranger was going to come into the bathroom with me and my sisters furious that we were together, yelling at us to get out and go to our separate prostitution rooms. It meant being in my unaltered state of teenage mind, where I could be consumed with hearing my favorite song on the radio, not daydreaming about simply laying on my bed in peace. It meant having food, real food, when I was hungry versus having my stomach crammed with tiny pills that could make my heart stop, washed down with liquor I was far too young to drink, and thrown a hamburger or two. It meant being with my little brother, who I yearned to get on my nerves, and my mother, who was often preoccupied with him, but who would not hurt or ridicule me.

Imagining home that happy, secure place was different than actually being back there. After those few weeks, I was a changed girl. A girl, who thought I'd become a woman. I did not emerge unscathed. We, all three of us, were changed for the worse. We'd seen the wilds of the world and could not turn back the hands of time in our memories. There was no going back to the way things were. Does a soldier return home the same as before he marched off to war? Neither did we.

It would be years before the sound of a door closing wouldn't make me stare at the doorway of the room I was in as if Squeaky was going to come swinging through it. The reek of the house would not leave my nostrils for a long, long time. Neither would the scent of the nasty, street men, the kind who don't take care of their personal hygiene or care to rape young girls. Hearing the lullaby, 'London Bridges' would be one that haunted me for the rest of my life.

Even in a place where I should have found such comfort and solace, I could not. I did not feel safe at home. I did not feel safe at school. I only felt safe with my sisters. Running away became my thing. Maybe because I'd run away from Squeaky and that house so many times in my mind, I was just on the run. Literally and figuratively.

My mom didn't know how to handle my running away. I'd run away to Jessica's house often. My mom didn't like it; however, she didn't fight me as much as she could have. She knew if I was with Jessica, I was safe and she could easily put her hands on me versus me just being out running the streets. Cell phones were nowhere near as common as they are now, especially for kids. A few of us had pagers and that was the most. So, there was no way for my mom to keep tabs on my comings and goings. At least not giving me a hard time about being with Jessica, she could pick up the phone and call me or talk to Jessica's grandparents who'd just seen me and knew where I was.

Jessica respected her grandparents and they respected her. Whereas my mom treated me like a teenager, Nana and Papa treated Jessica like an adult. My mom would look at me sideways, "Oh, I know you're not walking in this house at 2:00 in the morning at 12 years old!" and go off on me. Nana and Papa wouldn't do that to Jessica. In my eyes, she was grown and I desired to have that level of freedom she had.

One day, Papa dropped us off at the flea market to hang out. We walked around to see what we could spend our little money on. Out of nowhere, Jessica grabbed my arm and turned to me with eyes the size of golf balls. "We gotta go."

"Why?" I asked slightly irritated.

"We have to get out of here. Squeaky is here!" My mind instantly went back to hearing him yell that he was going to kill her. Squeaky threatened Jessica often; he didn't talk to me or Nicole that way. After the two of them had the big fight, he always told her he was going to kill her. It was one of the first things he said to her any time she fixed her mouth like she was thinking about rebelling.

"We are good, Jessica. Chill out."

"No man! We gotta go…NOW!" she was emphatic and beelined for the door. I don't know if she caught a glimpse of him, smelled him, heard his voice, or was just terrified by the ghost of his presence. She was convinced he was in that building. We had to leave.

A few years later, around 15 years old, I was involved in an altercation at my job behind Squeaky. I worked at a daycare center and one of the children in my class was related to Squeaky. He was the child's father's uncle. The child's father came to pick the child up and when we locked eyes, I knew something wasn't right. Apparently, he felt it, too. We both looked away, then looked back at each other. The light bulbs went off in our heads at the same time. He bashfully turned his head away from me, got his child and scurried out. He was one of the guys who paid Squeaky to have his way with us. It was amazing that as high and drunk as they kept us and as much as I tried not to look in the men's eyes, I remembered him.

Not too long after, the child's mother and a car full of her friends rolled up on me at my job as I was leaving. "Jessica!" They called me to the car. As I said before, I was used to being mistaken for her. That had been happening since we met.

"I'm not Jessica, I'm Tatiana. What's up?"

"Yeah, you can get it, too! You put our people in jail! We owe you an ass whoopin' for that!" the passenger yelled out of the window as they spilled out of the car.

"First of all, your people raped us. You have daughters, right? You have kids...daughters? I was 12 years old! He raped me! He took my virginity! How would you feel if somebody raped your daughter? If you wanna fight me, come fight me! We can get it on right here. But I will not apologize for putting somebody in jail who raped me and sold my body!"

They backed up; their faces were shocked. I'm sure that was not the response they were anticipating. They rolled up on me five, six deep ready for a fight. They did not anticipate me standing up to them owning my truth. It hurt me. Even though time distanced me from the event, three years later I was faced with having to fight to defend myself against what he had done to me. And the level of ignorance that those women carried with them, not thinking about themselves or their kids being in that same situation to the point that they would track down a teenage girl at her job. It was beyond me.

With them knowing where I worked, it added a heightened level of nervousness to my day-to-day routine. At any moment, he could have come up to my job to retaliate or sent somebody else who couldn't be talked down. Once again, I feared for my life.

So much of that time spent being kidnapped and held by Squeaky was behind me. I could try my damnedest to push it out of my head and try to forget it. I could pretend I wasn't jittery and overly cautious about my actions. Yet, still, at any point, I could be faced with the ugly reminders of the darkest period of my life.

nineteen

NICOLE

"We're moving to California," my mom announced matter-of-factly. She told me she met a new guy and they'd decided to move in together. Well, she was moving into his place. It was an odd situation, she'd only just met this guy on the internet and was preparing to move us in with him.

We flew across the country from Jacksonville to Cali to begin anew. I knew I would miss my sisters, but putting space between me and Squeaky would be a good move. Being in a new city was the epitome of a new start. The change of scenery was the perfect pivot to keep me from seeing reminders of the grueling experience I'd had.

My mom's new boo had a small apartment. I looked around and noticed there was only one bedroom. "Where am I going to stay? Where's my room?" I asked.

"We're gonna go to dinner at your great-aunt's house." Not paying any attention that she didn't answer my question, I was agreeable. We all hopped in his car and drove the hour distance from the small town we were in to San Francisco where my great-aunt lived. My thoughts were that we would eat and go back to our new digs. However, as my mom said her goodbyes, her new boo brought my suitcase into my great-aunt's living room.

"Why is my stuff here?" I asked my mom. She could not even look at me. As I stared at her waiting on a response, her gaze turned away from mine.

"Well, honey, you're going to stay here for a while," my great-aunt said.

"Mom! Why is my suitcase here? Why are you leaving me here? What is she talking about?" My mom offered no explanation. She just left. Off to start her new life with her new boo, without her daughter.

My great-aunt showed me the room where I would be staying and told me to get settled in. I was staying with her teenage daughter. My cousin slept on the top bunk, I slept on the bottom. There I was, one year removed from being kidnapped and my mother was abandoning me...again. Nothing anybody could have said to me at that time would have made me feel any better about the situation. I felt like she didn't look for me as hard as she should have when I was missing. She dropped me off at a group home. Now, she was choosing a new man over me, leaving me with my great-aunt in an unfamiliar city where I had no friends and no immediate family in another sneaky operation situation.

I stared off into the distance that night trying to find sleep. I was sad, hurt, angry, betrayed, rejected. It was all too much. At least she didn't leave me with a complete stranger, which at that point I didn't put it past her. Luckily, my California family visited Florida often and vice versa, so I was close to my great-aunt and her kids.

My great-aunt worked at the school where she

enrolled me. She was lenient enough on me where I didn't feel like I was in a claustrophobic situation, but strict enough to offer discipline. All of the kids had chores. She expected me to go to school and do well. She taught me how to drive. As a person, she treated me well, checked on my transition in school often, was helpful and kind to me. Yet, she didn't know that I had been kidnapped and raped. Back then, I was not aware of that.

It was much different than being at home with my mom who never checked on my schooling or schoolwork. Nor did she give me affection. It was so foreign seeing my great-aunt hug her children and tell them she loved them, and for her to hug on me as well. Finally receiving that type of attention from a mother figure was so refreshing. I was excited to do the chores and go to school. I had no problem pulling my share of the weight in the house.

After about a month of living there and getting adjusted to my new life, my routine changed. Her husband started picking me up from school. He started getting handsy with me. He'd ask me how my day went with a heavy, clammy hand resting on my thigh. It was awkward and weird, but he kept doing it even when I flinched and pulled away.

His advances took a giant leap when he came into my bedroom one night. I was terrified. I still hadn't gotten completely used to my new surroundings and wasn't quite used to sharing a room. My uncle, a huge man both big and tall like Michael Clarke Duncan from *The Green Mile*, crept into my bedroom with a knife in his hand. Before I could react, he reached his hand up to the bed on the top bunk touching his daughter. I was confused about what was happening; even more confused with why this massive man needed a knife to walk into our room.

After doing whatever he was doing to her on the top bunk, he spread some of his 'love' down to me on the bottom. I guess he didn't want me to be feel left out. He pulled back the covers and touched me. My body froze. I stopped breathing. The overwhelming feeling of dread filled my belly. *NOOOOOOO!* I screamed inside. I couldn't believe this was happening to me. Again. I'd finally found a place that felt like home and he ripped the carefree feeling away from me.

I didn't know what to do or who to tell. Why

would I tell? After hearing the way my mom talked about me to people, I was sure my aunt wouldn't have believed me anyway. I was too scared to say anything. As if he sensed the ramblings of my mind trying to figure out a move or waiting to let out a scream, he whispered, "I'll kill you and I'll kill your auntie. Don't fuck with me." The outside floodlights caught a glint off the steel from the knife's blade as if reinforcing his threat. I'd been in the face of danger before and did not take kindly to threats.

Soon, he was coming in every night. That was not going to work for me. I began running away, skipping school. My behavior only reinforced the picture my mom painted of me to my aunt. Going to school meant my uncle was going to be picking me up, which meant more time for us to be alone. That gave him more sick feels and more time to threaten me. It also gave him more time to go even further.

Running away, I met Michael, a nice guy who offered me a place to stay and a way to make money. This was it for me. If I couldn't trust my mom and couldn't trust living in the house with my great-aunt and her husband, I might as well forge a new life completely on my own. "You can come stay with me. You gotta make some money tho; you gotta get on the track." Being young and naïve, I didn't realize he was a pimp and the track meant I'd be selling myself.

He wasn't forceful about it, but was upfront, "If you wanna hang out with me, that is what you gotta do."

Truthfully, by that point, I didn't care anymore. I would willingly do almost anything to keep from having to go back to that house. Before going to my great-aunt's house, I hadn't had many interactions with men. My father wasn't around. The men my mom dated were here today, gone tomorrow. They could barely take interest in forming a relationship because my mom kept them away from me and in a revolving door.

Between Squeaky, my uncle, and now Michael, I figured this was just how men operated. In the situation with Michael, if I was going to be taken advantage of, at least I would be making money to take care of myself instead of someone making money off of me or having their way with me.

My great-aunt had been with him for a number of years by that point. Clearly, whatever he was doing to me, he was doing to his own daughter. Either my great-aunt was turning a deaf ear or she didn't know. I convinced myself that my pleas would go unanswered and I would probably put both of our lives in jeopardy.

I finally mustered up the courage to tell somebody about the abuse at my great-aunt's house. I told her son, who was an older, male cousin, my uncle had been touching me. What shocked me was that his response was not one of surprise. It was more of, "Mmm hmm." I looked at him puzzled. As if reading my confusion, he confessed, "You know what? I'm sorry, cuz. My sister said the same thing about him and my mom didn't do shit about it."

BOOM! That sent my world spinning. Why the hell would my mom send me to live with them in the first place? Why would my great-aunt invite me into their home knowing full well what her husband was capable of and would more than likely do? What kind of loving, protective environment was I in? All of a sudden, I was scared all over again. Scared and repulsed. I would receive no support in this situation.

Needless to say, it wasn't a nice move-out situation. The police were called, they took my uncle away in cuffs. I went to the police station to give a full statement, on camera. It was daunting. My uncle was released for reasons unbeknownst to me. I was too young at 14 to understand what was going on with the investigation and I didn't care either. I just wanted out! Out of the house! Out of the situation!

My great-aunt threw her wild accusations at me insinuating, "You probably seduced my husband! I don't know where you're going, but you can't stay here anymore!" In her heart, she knew the truth. I wasn't the first person to say they were touched by him. Her own daughter spilled the beans on him. If it was easy to turn her back on her daughter, I knew she was going to do the same to me. She packed my clothes, drove me to the train station, gave me $2 and put me out.

I caught up with Michael and asked him to come get me. He did and that was that. The most painful part of everything was my mother didn't try to save me. She didn't try to help me. She never seemed to care that I'd been put out of my great-aunt's house. Michael put me on the track. I officially became a prostitute.

Twenty

The room erupted in applause. Filled with teenage girls, their mothers and caretakers, and advocates for sexual justice, there was a mixed bag of responses. Some were crying, others had their hands over their chests, while still others were beaming from ear-to-ear. The young lady who escorted them into the room approached Tatiana and Nicole as they stood on the stage.

"I have a question," a young girl boldly stood up as the applause was dying down. She looked to be around 15.

"Sure!" Nicole said giving a warm smile.

"Where is Jessica?"

She asked the question that was on so many minds. Nicole looked to her side to her partner as they mentally decided who was going to answer.

"I'll take it," Tatiana said. "As you know, Nicole was moved to California shortly after we broke free. Jessica and I became thick as thieves," Tatiana laughed. "Unfortunately, she was killed in 2017. Because Squeaky made so many threats against her life, he was the first person I thought of when I heard she'd been murdered. Sadly, her murder is still unsolved. Squeaky was sentenced to four years in prison for what he did to us, but he didn't serve all of his time. He may have served a year and some change. He was killed in 2018."

"For me," Tatiana began, "life outside the game began after Jessica was murdered. Living life outside of the game was one of the biggest transitions I'd ever made in my life. Experiencing what I'd been through because of the life I'd been thrust into, I felt a young death was my only end. I thought I'd end up like her. I had come to the point where I was ok with dying. But, I wanted to live! I started to make changes; not anything big, just to live beyond 18. The seeds that were sown while I was in courted-ordered programs, such as the truancy program, helped to save my life. I hated every minute of being in those lock-down facilities and could not make sense of being surrounded by girls like me who, talked about our experiences. Of course, things rarely make sense when you're going through them. Then, there was the *aha* moment! It took years for Nicole and I to realize that we had not just been raped, but trafficked. Sexually exploited. From there, we saw a need to equip people with warning signs by telling our story. Recognizing there are so many women and, young girls especially, who this has happened to...is happening to, helped me to understand there is a greater purpose for my life. That is why I'm still here."

Tatiana took a deep breath before continuing. "I am not ashamed of what happened to us. I am strong enough to put one foot in front of the other. I'm brave enough to walk alongside another survivor who isn't quite to the point of accepting their past and moving forward. Our hope is that God will help people get whatever they need from our story. I firmly believe our

God knows what we need and he will provide that for us."

The room erupted again. The sound was thunderous with cheering and clapping from some 200 attendees.

"The way I was able to escape the life completely came after being invited to church. There, I met a woman who had a similar background in that she'd also been trafficked. We sat next to each other and got to know one another. I learned a lot from her, she's now my survivor mentor. Through that church, I was able to get baptized and find myself. The growth I experienced as a result led me into the work I do know which is advocacy for young ladies. I encourage them that it's never to late to go back to school, while also helping them navigate their feelings knowing they are not alone. Tatiana and I now lead support groups and help organizations that assist survivors in understanding and whole-heartedly believing there is life outside the game."

"We want to thank Tatiana and Nicole for generously sharing their stories with us. And what powerful stories they were! We are so happy that you ladies are still alive and well. You are mothers now, who give back to the sex and human trafficking community by being shining pillars of the world through your testimony. You have no idea how much it means for us to see you standing here to show us there is victory after being a victim; we can survive and thrive!" she offered beginning another round of clapping.

The room started clapping again. Tatiana and Nicole joined hands. "Any other questions?" Nicole asked. Hands went up around the room.

THE END

Human Trafficking Defined...

Human trafficking is modern day slavery and involves the use of *force, fraud or coercion* to obtain some type of labor or commercial sex act.

Adults and minors of sex trafficking according to the law:

- Adults are deemed victims of criminal sex trafficking when they are exploited into a commercial sex act through *force, fraud or coercion.*
- Minors (under age 18) are deemed victims of criminal sex trafficking when they are persuaded into a commercial sex act, regardless of whether *force, fraud or coercion* are used.

Human trafficking victims and survivors of trafficking come from all walks of life. People harmed by human trafficking are diverse. Anyone can be trafficked.

Traffickers prey upon people with the following characteristics or experiences by offering to meet some kind of physical or emotional need, thereby gaining control over that person.

Common circumstances in vulnerable populations:

- Minors
- Runaway youth
- Low self-esteem, depression
- History of sexual abuse, physical abuse or other trauma
- Parent or guardian has substance abuse issues
- College students, junior/high school students

Sex Trafficking RED FLAGS

Recognizing key indicators of human trafficking is the first step in identifying victims of human trafficking and can help save a life.

- Lying about age, fake ID
- Frequently missing school/falling asleep in school
- Hotel room keys
- Restricted communication, no eye contact
- Older boyfriend, dominating boyfriend
- Large amounts of cash
- Sudden dramatic change in behavior
- Seems fearful, timid
- Has brandings/tattoo display "daddy"
- Inappropriate clothing for the weather or venue
- Uses slang or code words used in the commercial sex industry
- Disconnected from family, friends, or house of worship
- Doesn't know what day of the week it is
- Appears to be coached on what to say

30% of human trafficking victims are children

If you notice any signs of human trafficking please call your local authorities or the

Human Trafficking Hotline

1-888-373-7888

To become a certified anti human trafficking advocate visit **unitedtraffickingjustice.teachable.com** to learn more.

Are you being groomed?

Grooming is a stage in the recruitment process. A pimp/trafficker can be a man or a woman; young or old. Most pimps use manipulation to lure potential victims. They may even use another person to do this manipulation before you're even introduced to the pimp/trafficker.

The pimp will appear as a friend or boyfriend/ girlfriend. They might be the only person who really listens to you and that's only because they are listening to know your vulnerabilities. The pimp will find out your dreams and ambitions or their frustrations and pains. Then, they will offer a way out of the pain in your life, or a way to reach your dreams.

The pimp/trafficker will use many tactics to lure his victims.

Here are some warning signs to watch out for:

- Taking you shopping/giving you gifts
- Wine and dining you
- Providing you with things you want/need
- Taking you on trips

- Photoshoot for "modeling casting calls"
- Giving you small amounts drugs to eventually get you hooked
- Suggests ways to make fast money
- Uses other girls to invite you out to hang or go clubbing
- Asks you to invite your friends to come hang out with you and him/her

And for teen boys, some traffickers use video games to lure them in. So, please be aware if you are asked to send a photo of yourself online.

Force

- Forceful drug introduction
- Rape
- Imprisonment
- Physical Abuse

Fraud

- Fake model casting call/job
- Romeo pimp (deceitful romance), pretends to be a boyfriend

- Fake promises of a better life
- Black mail

Coercion

- Manipulation
- Controlling
- Threatening violence to a victim or their family
- Relationship is based on fear
- Setting daily quotas
- Making victim believe they deserve to be victimized

Victims of human trafficking are deprived of the most basic human right: the right to FREEDOM.

Trafficking victims are often forced into sex work by guerilla pimps or coerced by a romeo pimp and are now feeling stuck in a life of dehumanizing work. It is a crime that affects people from all over the world, including the United States.

If you or someone you know is being trafficked or may be being groomed by a trafficker, please reach out to Survivor Advocates Nicole McCall & Tatiana Yoguez at...

www.lifeoutsidethegame.com

Keep in touch!

@iamtatianayoguez

@iamnicolemccall

Made in the USA
Columbia, SC
13 July 2021

41737134R00112